The Writing Teacher's Troubleshooting Guide

- Nothing to write about
- Exploring a topic
- Finding a vision
- Finding a focus
- Developing a lead
- Establishing a context
- Wandering off on a tangent
- Controlling details
- Bringing closure
- Resisting revision
- Considering conventions

Lester L. Laminack and Reba M. Wadsworth

Heinemann
Portsmouth, NH

Heinemann

361 Hanover Street

Portsmouth, NH 03801–3912

www.heinemann.com

Offices and agents throughout the world

Library of Congress Cataloging-in-Publication Data

Laminack, Lester L.

   The writing teacher's troubleshooting guide / Lester L. Laminack and Reba M. Wadsworth.

     pages   cm

   Includes bibliographical references.

   ISBN: 978-0-325-04341-8

   1. Creative writing (Elementary education). 2. English language—Composition and exercises—Study and teaching (Elementary). I. Wadsworth, Reba M. II. Title.

LB1576.L255 2013

372.62'3—dc23   2013016081

Editor: Holly Kim Price

Production: Victoria Merecki

Cover design: Matthew Simmons

Front cover photos: © wanchai/Shutterstock.com and Getty Images/HIP

Interior design: Bernadette Skok

Typesetter: Kim Arney

Manufacturing: Steve Bernier

Printed in the United States of America on acid-free paper

17 16 15 14 13 VP 1 2 3 4 5

We dedicate this book to

Zachary Seth Laminack *and*
Christina Wadsworth Bishop

Table of Contents

Acknowledgments

The ideas for this guide bounced around in our minds long before the first words appeared on a computer screen. Each time one of us left a group of teachers we picked up the phone and called the other. Our conversations tended to drift toward recurring concerns of teachers of writing and how we responded to those concerns. Of course, during those conversations we could think of suggestions we could have offered, resources we should have recommended . . . could have . . . should have . . . . Then one afternoon we decided to begin keeping track of those recurring concerns and make note of how teachers addressed them. The result is in your hands. We are grateful to the numerous teachers who have nudged our thinking by trusting us enough to share their struggles, especially the literacy coaches and teachers of Cobb County, GA under the guidance of Dianna Denton, the teachers of The University School at East Tennessee State University, the teachers of Francine Delaney New School for Children, and the teachers of Monroe County Schools, MS.

This project was a pleasure to write and that is in no small way due to the supportive team of folks at Heinemann. Kate Montgomery met the idea with interest and enthusiasm. Zoe Ryder White helped us fine-tune the format to stay true to our desire to model this after a vintage VW Beetle troubleshooting guide. Our editor, Holly Kim Price, was there at every turn offering her insights and guidance. Matthew Simmons and Bernadette Skok gave life to our vision through their design work for the cover and interior. Victoria Merecki was the shepherd who led the manuscript through production. We are grateful to each of you.

And we are grateful to have the support of Ryan Ammons and Mike Wadsworth who are there for us always.

Introduction

The Writing Teacher's Troubleshooting Guide is intended as an efficient reference designed to provide a handful of quick, easily implemented ideas for nudging growth when students pause on the cusp of development or rest on a plateau of safety. The format of this guide is loosely based on the "Troubleshooting Guide" found in VW Beetles during the 1970s. The appeal of this format is its clear, concise, and practical design.

The VW troubleshooting guide was organized in three columns and presented over a few pages of the owner's manual. The left column presented a situation owners may experience in the operation of the vehicle. The center column presented possible causes for that situation. And the right column offered possible solutions for the owner to try:

If your vehicle . . .   This may be   Try this . . .
                             happening because . . .

This clean, simple design appeals to us. It nudges us to consider the patterns of growth, pauses, and plateaus developing writers experience along the way. The spare design compels us to think and to pare down our language to the bare essentials. It requires the practical.

By its very design a troubleshooting guide is intended to create ease of use, to build both the competence and confidence of the user. That is our goal in selecting this format. First we name an issue teachers have seen a writer struggle with (notice and name). Then, we pose a few possible reasons for that pause or plateau in the student's development as a writer (identify cause). And in the next column we offer a few possibilities for nudging growth (give the writer tools to move forward).

Teachers of writing have experiences that enable us to recognize patterns of growth and moments of struggle and confusion; pauses in development and idle periods where developing writers rely on what is safe. We know that a writer can grow if we recognize when and how to nudge, to demonstrate, to lead, or to stand back for a moment. This guide, then, draws on the experiences of teachers in identifying typical patterns of struggle, pause, and confusion among developing writers.

It is our intention to be as clear and concise as possible. We strive to be as practical and immediately applicable as we can. In addition to offering possible causes for the situation observed and some possible ways to nudge growth, we also include suggested mentor texts for some situations. These texts are not necessary to implement the suggestions. Rather, they are offered as yet another resource busy teachers may bring into the instructional cycle. We suggest these mentor texts be used in a variety of ways: to launch a study within the writing workshop, to demonstrate or provide an example of a writer's ways of working, to be paired with examples from the teacher or developing writers, as part of a minilesson with the whole class, to demonstrate on the spot when conferring with one writer, and as an example when working with a small group.

When using this guide please note we offer *possible* causes and *possible* solutions. There is no "one-size-fits-all" solution. We also recognize there is rarely (if ever) a "one-shot" fix for anything in writing and that when working with individuals you must consider many factors. Therefore, our suggestions are an attempt to lead the writer one step forward.

As in any troubleshooting guide, the suggestions are *possibilities* or *options* to try out. The intent here is to lead writing teachers toward thinking of development with a different lens that may lead to a clearer understanding of the developmental nature of language and literacy learning.

Teachers recognize that often you need to teach the same idea a dozen times in a dozen different ways before a child is able to incorporate it into his or her independent writing. Sometimes an instructional nudge may move the writer forward in one piece, yet may not hold across time, whereas in other instances, one exposure changes everything for the writer. So, we encourage you to view each instructional nudge as one more demonstration of what writers do when facing a struggle. Work alongside your students, and support their growing control and developing competence with repeated exposures layered over time. Note what you observe, what puzzles you, why you believe the snag has happened. Note what you try in an attempt to nudge the writer forward.

Each of the suggestions for nudging growth is intended to support an individual child; however, we suggest you consider the possibility that many of these suggestions could also be used with small groups, and several will be appropriate as the focus of a minilesson during writing workshop. In fact, you will likely find these suggestions could be used in a spiraling fashion.

We think of spiraling in two ways. The first is to spiral the use of a strategy from an individual to a small group or the entire class. In this case you may see the situation with one child, take a suggested action, then monitor and begin noticing the same pause or plateau with others, a group, or the whole class. In these cases you may return to the same "if/then" situations several times. Each time you return to the situation you increase the potential in the writer, group, or class. Each time you work through the situation you help the writers to broaden their understandings and control as they move onward.

Spiraling may also mean that you use one of the suggestions and find it moves the writer forward in a particular unit of study. You may find that the writer does not carry over the suggestion to a new unit of study. We suggest that you then loop back to the if/then situation, employ the same or different suggestion to lift the writer again, spiraling upward (as we move through units of study and time) and outward (as the writer broadens

his or her understanding and begins to generalize that a single move can apply to more than one type of writing).

We are including several mentor texts that we have found useful in developing our insights as writers and teachers of writing. It is our hope that, as you plan and implement your writing workshop, these mentor texts will be a helpful resource. In addition, we have added a glossary of selected terms that are frequently tossed about in conversations about writing. It has been our experience that terms can quickly become part of the professional conversation. However, those terms may hold rather different meanings in different schools, or even across classrooms within the same school. We include the glossary with our meaning for the words we use. Our suggestion is that you take a look at the words you use in your teaching and your talking about teaching writing. Have some professional conversations with colleagues to define what is meant by the words we use as we teach. Otherwise it is possible that children will rise through the grades hearing common terms that mean one thing in second grade and something else in fourth. Pin down what you mean, and let definitions expand as children gain proficiency in the art and work of writing.

As teachers and writers, our insights and understandings continue to grow as we work in classrooms, attend workshops and conferences, and read professional literature. Over the years we have found a wealth of ideas and suggestions in the writing of others that have nudged our thinking. Therefore, we are including a list of professional books that have been especially helpful to growing our knowledge and deepening our insights. We group these titles to target specific issues and hope they provide an opportunity for more in-depth study leading to greater insight about your work.

We invite you to use this book as a troubleshooting guide. Read it once all the way through. Get a feel for what's inside and how it's organized. Then, keep it handy for those times when one of your developing writers has a temporary developmental pause or just an off morning.

All the best,
Lester and Reba

Nothing to Write About

1

When given the task to write, less experienced writers may immediately respond, "But I don't know anything. . . . I don't know what to write about. . . . What do you want me to write about?" Those words are all too familiar in classrooms everywhere. As a teacher it would be easy to fall prey to the fear and simply respond with a prompt or an assigned topic. While this may produce writing and appear to solve the dilemma, it doesn't get at the root of the problem. In fact, it may make matters worse because it 1) erodes the potential of learning to value and trust one's own experiences and thoughts as source material, 2) moves the writer even further from understanding the source of inspiration, 3) undermines the development of a habit of noticing and taking note with the intention of generating source material for future projects, and 4) weakens the association between the writer's passions and experience with the act of writing.

To work consistently from a prompt could create writing in an emotional vacuum where what the writer produces has its origins in the heart and head of someone else.

The spark for writing is rarely something that can happen on demand, so it comes as no surprise that some students routinely respond with, "I don't know what to write about." Learning to attend to the world around you and to tune in to the potential in what you notice, like many other aspects of writing, must become habit. Writers often speak about where their ideas come from (family, comments overheard, situations observed, music heard, books read, experiences). A common thread running through those comments is the writer's attentive nature. Writers are an attentive lot who tune in to the potential of their noticing. As a writer I (Lester) keep a notebook and jot down ideas that flash through my mind, capturing only enough of the idea to ignite the memory and launch future writing. It is the potential I am trying to capture here. The act of writing it down tickles my brain and causes me to think around the edges of that potential topic. At odd moments I will have some insight, or an image will drift through my mind, and I turn to my notebook to capture those fleeting thoughts. Over time, if these bits begin to coalesce, I move out of the notebook and attempt to draft.

My point here is this: "I don't know what to write about" may be the truth for many student writers if we are expecting students to come up with a topic on the spot just because we have announced an assignment.

A springboard experience (trigger event, seed idea, or source idea) sets the mind in motion and generates a cascade of thoughts and details that may find their way into the writing. Or at the very least it becomes the spark that ignites the connections and questions that later drive the writing. These moments are perfect material for writers to capture in a notebook because they can come from almost anywhere. Consider the potential in typical school-day experiences: During a morning read-aloud writers listen with notebooks open and make note of connections that spark memories or generate questions and curiosity. On the way to the playground a group of kids stop to watch a line of ants marching single file with crumbs from a dropped cookie. Questions shower like raindrops. Conjecture clouds the air. Conversations spark throughout the play. Later, in the lunchroom, a few peas slide off a tray and land on the floor. Moments later someone steps on those peas and slides into the person in front of him. A chain of disaster ensues. It becomes the topic of talk for a week. Back in the classroom a discussion erupts following a read-aloud of an Underground Railroad story connected to a social studies lesson. Comments ping around the room like hailstones, and questions bounce about. Ordinary life experience in a school is rich with potential ideas for gathering material. The attentive mind of a writer zeroes in on all that potential. And if student writers are taught to attend to this, the habit will spill over into life outside of school.

The key here is to note those events that capture our attention. Especially important are those ideas that prompt us to think, to question, to feel, to laugh, to share, to react, to take a stand—in short, those ideas that nudge us forward. Stories and poems, narratives and accounts, essays and letters and memoirs, opinion pieces, how-to and all-about texts, ABC books, and concept books are waiting to sprout from those seeds. But first they must be gathered, planted in our notebooks, then nurtured and cultivated with thought, talk, play, reading, writing, and more writing.

Identify Cause

The writer lacks experience noticing and assigning significance to ideas sparked by the world around her.

Give the Writer Tools to Move Forward

- Select a book that is likely to spark several connections. Read the book aloud with the student, and note the connections that may lead to a story, evoke an opinion, or elicit a response.

Mentor text:
Nothing Ever Happens on 90th Street by Roni Schotter

- Lead an idea walk with notebooks. Gather your students with their notebooks. Give them a focus (such as signs of the arrival of fall) to notice and make note of. Their noticings may be sketches, lists, words, phrases, first lines, smells, memories, or connections/associations. Pause along the walk to share what you have collected, and invite others to do the same. Speak of the potential of what you have noted.

Mentor texts:
Leaf Man by Lois Ehlert
The Dandelion Seed by Joseph P. Anthony
I Love the Rain by Margaret Park Bridges

- Listen to conversations. Show an entry in your own notebook that was prompted by an overheard conversation.

- Listen to music, and read the liner notes. List your favorite line, and add your comments, thoughts, connections, and so on. Make a list of ideas prompted by the song.

- Listen to TV/radio news or scan news magazines, and note what captures your attention. Note your thoughts, feelings, reactions, questions, differences of opinion, and so on.

- Sort through a collection of photographs, and make notes about the place, why you were there, who is in the picture, what is important to remember, and what the story is.

Identify Cause

The writer has little confidence in the worthiness of his ideas or is dependent on others for topic selection.

Give the Writer Tools to Move Forward

- Watch and listen to the student throughout the day, pointing out to him each of the things he says or does that could spark writing. Examples might include comments about favorite things, opinions shared, hopes and aspirations, connections with a read-aloud, moments when he has a spontaneous story to share, differences of opinion, questions that arise in science or social studies lessons, and concerns voiced over issues in the classroom, school, or community.

- Recall an event the student has shared. Retell a portion of that event, and pause to question him about details, the sequence, and why it was significant for him. Invite him to continue the telling to you. Make note of details on a sticky note, and hand it to him. Lead him to recognize the potential that lies in that list.

- Interview him for details about moments when he felt proud of himself, times when he was disappointed in others, or events that left him unable to stop laughing. Make note of details that may spark a story in his mind. Find out what makes him angry, what he is passionate about, and so on.

Mentor texts:
The Roller Coaster Kid by Mary Ann Rodman
First Grade Stinks! by Mary Ann Rodman

Identify Cause

The writer does not recognize her own emotions as a source of ideas for writing.

 ## Give the Writer Tools to Move Forward

- Make lists in your notebook (for example: what frightens you, what makes you laugh, what makes you worry, what makes you sad, what gets you excited). When you need a topic, think about something from your list, and tell why or write about a time when . . .

Mentor texts:
Rabbit Ears by Amber Stewart
Trevor's Wiggly-Wobbly Tooth by Lester L. Laminack

- Make an entry in your notebook to tell what you are feeling when you are flooded with emotion, such as after a great game on the playground, following a disappointment, when anticipating the visit of a grandparent or cousin from out of town, when you are thinking about a party, or the day before a visit to your dentist.

- Attach artifacts into your notebook (post cards, tickets, advertisements, news clips, photos or illustrations from magazines or newspapers, short essays), and add captions to note your thoughts, reactions, feelings, connections, questions, or arguments related to each.

Mentor texts:
My Rotten Redheaded Older Brother by Patricia Polacco
Dad, Jackie, and Me by Myron Uhlberg

- Consider personal collections or "treasures." Select one or more of them to describe; tell where it came from or how you acquired it and how you feel when you think of it or see it.

Mentor texts:
Treasures of the Heart by Alice Ann Miller
The Memory String by Eve Bunting

Identify Cause

The writer does not recognize that the people in his life can be a source of ideas for writing.

Give the Writer Tools to Move Forward

- Make a list of people you know really well (parents, siblings, extended family, neighbors, and friends). Leave a little space between each name on the list, and make notes about each person. To get you started, choose one and think about why that person is important to you, things you enjoy doing with the person, what makes you think of this person (e.g., smells, a color, a song, food), something this person always says, or a good memory shared with that person.

Mentor texts:
Saturdays and Teacakes by Lester L. Laminack
Song and Dance Man by Karen Ackerman

- Paste photos in your writer's notebook, and make notes telling where you are, who is with you, and what you were thinking when you were there. Focus on the people in the photos, and write down your memories with those people.

- Make notes and lists about a visit with grandparents, friends, or neighbors. Think about the people at a birthday party or other celebration you have attended. Is there one who stands out in your memory? Why? Make notes about what you can remember.

Mentor texts:
Mr. George Baker by Amy Hest
Bigmama's by Donald Crews

- Write or sketch a scene from a visit with a relative during a holiday or celebration such as birthdays, anniversaries, holidays, or vacations.

Mentor texts:
The Relatives Came by Cynthia Rylant
Grandma's Records by Eric Velasquez

Identify Cause

The writer does not recognize that significant places in her life can be a source of ideas.

Give the Writer Tools to Move Forward

- Make a list of places you have enjoyed visiting (amusement park, hiking trail, seashore, museum, aquarium, favorite store, bakery, campground, lake, grandparent's home, and so on). Make notes of what you recall—waiting in line, anticipations, smells, sounds, fears, worries, or excitement.

Mentor texts:
Bigmama's by Donald Crews
Roller Coaster by Marla Frazee
Picnic in October by Eve Bunting

- Make lists in your notebook of places you've been, places you'd love to go, or places you want to know more about. For each place listed, write whatever comes to mind.

Mentor text:
Tulip Sees America by Cynthia Rylant

Exploring a Topic

2

When a seed idea has been selected, few writers are equipped to jump right into the draft, even though they may want to. Taking time to roam around what is known about the topic, to explore what others have written, to examine your motivation and interest, and to look at possibilities is important for creating a vision for the text. Donald Murray (1989) said, "I am involved with the subjects I write about long before I know I am going to write about them. And I am involved to a degree I cannot demand of my students. I am on duty twenty-four hours a day . . ."

In our classrooms with less experienced writers we may not be "on duty twenty-four hours a day," but we can certainly recognize the need for, and *make time for*, reading, observing, absorbing, connecting, thinking, and rehearsing as it relates to the topics our writers have an interest in and may develop a passion for pursuing. This may include collecting and reading a stack of texts including books, articles, poems, interviews, profiles, biographies, and websites related to the topic. It may include talking with a friend or relative to gather details or memories from another point of view. It may include an interview to sort out facts, to raise questions, or to consider other viewpoints. It may include surfing the web to see what others have written and how they have approached the topic. It may be as simple as making lists of random thoughts, sketching a scene to visualize their thoughts, writing a quick character sketch, compiling a bulleted list of details you want to remember, or jotting down snags of conversations that have surfaced while thinking and talking about what you'll write. No matter how you go about it, exploring the topic and your connections to it is critical to the clarity and focus you will bring to the draft and later to the revisions.

"[T]he best subjects are close to us; it is our individual vision of our shared, familiar world that the reader finds most informing and satisfying" (Murray 1990, 79). Perhaps then, one of our greatest challenges is leading our writers first to value themselves and others enough to believe that the ordinary events of one's own life can become extraordinary writing. To explore our lives, our questions, those things in the world that intrigue us may be the best work we do as writers.

Identify Cause

The writer does not understand the purpose or importance of exploring the topic prior to writing.

Give the Writer Tools to Move Forward

- Invite the writer to make a series of sketches to get her thoughts in order and determine where she may have gaps in her knowledge or understanding. Try folding a sheet of paper into six or eight boxes.

- Invite the writer to make a list of the information she considers important for the text. A quickly written list of ideas, facts, places, people, concerns, questions, impressions, and beliefs may be enough to zero in and find the focus that will lead to a vision for the text.

- Invite the writer to make a plan describing how she will proceed with this topic—What type of text will it be? What does she know that is like what she has in mind? Will she need to read other texts to deepen her knowledge of the topic? Will she need to read examples of other texts to determine the appropriate scope of her idea? Does she have a structure in mind that will hold her thinking?

- Explore a text (such as a book, article, poem, or menu) the writer is familiar with. Read the text together with eyes and ears for the knowledge held by the writer. Imagine the notebook pages that came before and during the writing of those texts.

Mentor texts:
Bats by Gail Gibbons
Bat Loves the Night by Nicola Davies
In November by Cynthia Rylant
Chrysanthemum by Kevin Henkes
Apt. 3 by Ezra Jack Keats

Identify Cause

The writer has not been taught how to explore a topic to determine his interest and understanding.

Give the Writer Tools to Move Forward

- Help the writer make a bubble map with the topic in the center. Each bubble extending out represents an event or fact to be explored. Examine the map to determine if there are gaps in knowledge or perhaps limited interest.

- Have the writer conduct an interview with someone who has more information—an authority, an older relative, a friend, or another staff member in the school to broaden perspective and determine an appropriate scope for the project.

- Assist the writer in collecting a small stack of resources or mentor texts to read. Note the various formats, structures, and text features available to the writer. This stack may be topic related if the intent is to grow knowledge, vocabulary, and insight. Or the stack may represent a variety of formats to offer possible "containers" for the writer's knowledge.

- Demonstrate the use of note cards or sticky notes to explore significance, collect information, and pose questions.

- Invite the writer to think about other texts he has read about the same topic. Explore the focus and scope of those texts.

- Invite the writer to make a timeline for events and list questions he hopes the reader could answer afterward. Use those questions to form an outline or create a structure.

Mentor text:
Saving Samantha by Robbyn van Frankenhuyzen

- List what you want the reader to know, understand, feel, think, challenge, and question. Consider how other texts have accomplished this, and plan for which you will bring into your writing.

Identify Cause

The writer does not have adequate background knowledge of the topic.

Give the Writer Tools to Move Forward

- Have the writer make a list of the facts he knows or believes to be true. Sit with the list, and talk through the sources of his knowledge. Lead him through collecting a set of texts that will enable him to verify his existing understandings, clarify his fuzzy thoughts, and develop new insights and questions to pursue before writing.

- Invite the writer to list the characters who will be in the text. Next to each character make notes about personality, appearance, attitude, words and phrases the character uses frequently, memorable traits, and significant details that will help the reader come to know the character as you do. (For example, John is the kind of guy who stops to help strangers, he loves the color blue, peanut butter, and pizza. If he had a choice of playing in the park with friends or sitting on the steps with a book, John would be reading.)

- Invite the writer to read a small collection of texts to add to his vocabulary and information. Keep the collection in a tub near where he writes. Demonstrate for him how writers pause to read, pose questions to themselves, make notes, and move between reading and writing in the development of a text.

- Bookmark a few websites for the writer to visit as a means of building background.

- Invite the writer to devote a few pages in his writer's notebook for gathering ideas, insights, wonderings, notes, and sketches.

- Revisit the writer's notebook with him. Talk together about topics of interest. Scaffold a conversation for one or two of these topics, helping him find an area of authority.

Opportunities for Study/Possible Mentor Texts

Either of the two options below could be done with an individual, a small group, or the entire class, depending on your intentions and the needs your writers exhibit. The idea here is to examine why and how writers need to take the time to explore their knowledge, vocabulary, insights, questions, and interest level before launching a project.

Nonfiction

The opportunity for study here is to investigate how writers use reading and research to explore a topic, generate new questions, deepen understanding, clarify vocabulary, and develop new ideas before launching into writing. These books have been gathered to provide an opportunity for exploring a nonfiction topic. We want students to discover how one title scaffolds for another and that with each new layer of complexity and depth an even greater understanding is needed—and that calls for further exploration of other source material.

Possible Texts for This Nonfiction Study

Ashley, Susan. 2004. *Ants* [Let's Read About Insects]. Pleasantville, NY: Weekly Reader Books.
Ashley, Susan. 2004. *Bees* [Let's Read About Insects]. Pleasantville, NY: Weekly Reader Books.

Sill, Cathryn. 2000. *About Insects: A Guide for Children.* Atlanta: Peachtree.
Taylor, Barbara. 2006. *Insects* [Science Kids]. New York: Kingfisher Publications.

Procedure

Present *About Insects* as a read-aloud. In the first read skip the afterword section. Invite the students to work in pairs to make an inventory of the information Cathryn includes. This should be a running list of facts (for example, insects have six legs, insects have three body parts, and antennae help insects smell and feel). Combine the inventory to create a master list. Note the information Cathryn had to gather before writing her book.

Return to the book for a second read-aloud. Pause when additional information needs to be added to the list. This time include the afterword. Note the additional, more detailed information included here. Flesh out those details with a second color on the list. Include the more detailed information alongside the appropriate "fact" from the original list.

Review the list and lead the group to think and talk about how Cathryn Sill learned so much about insects. Help them understand that her knowledge was essential to writing this book.

Present the other books on the list, showing how each of them has even more detailed and more specific information. Read a few samples from each, and note how reading books such as these could help a writer acquire the knowledge needed to write an all-about book.

Fiction

The opportunity here is to investigate how a writer of fiction taps into several possible sources of material to explore the topic before writing. It may well be personal experience and memory prompted by artifacts, photographs, or conversations and interviews with friends and family. It may be through reading other texts with a similar theme or topic, listening to music, or seeing a movie. Or it may be revisiting (either physically or through memory) the scene.

Possible Text for This Fiction Study

Crews, Donald. 1998. *Bigmama's*. New York: Greenwillow.

Procedure

Present *Bigmama's* as an uninterrupted read-aloud. As you reach the last page let your voice fade, close the book, and remain quiet and sit with the story a moment. Let them take it in. Then, invite them to talk with their partners about the book. After a few moments have them think about what Donald Crews may have needed to recall and make note of before writing this book. Imagine photos or artifacts he may have come across that tickled his memories and became entries in a notebook. Brainstorm other books with similar topics or themes that would spark your memories to write a book like this one.

Let's imagine a list of characters, places, or special memories he may have worked from. Show how that thinking and exploring may have made the writing more specific and organized.

Finding a Vision

3

Take a moment to recall your most recent vacation. Chances are you thought about it for a long time, making plans for where you would stay, mapping out the best way to get there, making a list of things to do, and choosing restaurants to try. You may have daydreamed a bit and pictured yourself already there, imagining how it would feel. When you arrived it is likely that many things occurred just as you had imagined. It is also likely that, for various reasons, some of those plans were revised on the spot as you lived through each day. A trip of some consequence, such as a vacation, is something most of us think about long before execution. The making of plans, the consideration of options, and the reasoning behind our decisions are all part of the vision we develop long before we pack the car to set out on the journey. A vision helps us organize and move forward, to anticipate, but it does not become a non-negotiable blueprint.

We want to lead developing writers toward just such thinking. We want them to not only think about what they are planning to write, not just the topic (for example, the time my sister fell off her bike and broke her arm) or even the sequence of events or plot (she got on her bike, pedaled out the drive, turned onto the street, and picked up speed) but also imagine what it will be like when it is written. That includes thinking about whether it will be a poem or report, an account, an essay, a feature article, an all-about book, a picture book, a cautionary tale, a menu, or a travel guide. That includes thinking about whether I write as if I am present and in the moment or assuming the role of narrator from afar. It also includes considering how the writing will progress from opening line to concluding statements, deciding what perspective to take, which tense to use, the role of the setting, and the genre. It includes thoughts about opening lines and possible endings. And it includes understanding *why* you are writing this and what you want the reader to know, understand, believe, or question.

William Zinsser (2001) reminds us, "[l]earning how to organize a long article is just as important as learning how to write a clear and pleasing sentence. All your clear and pleasing sentences will fall apart if you don't keep remembering that writing is linear and sequential, that logic is the glue that holds it together, that tension must be maintained from one sentence to the next and from one paragraph to the next and from one section to the next, and that narrative—good old-fashioned storytelling—is what should pull your readers along without their noticing the tug. The only thing they should notice is that you have made a sensible plan for your journey. Every step should seem inevitable" (265–266).

Finding a vision for the work comes through experience as a reader and as a listener to texts of all types on a range of topics. Annie Dillard (1989) notes, "[t]he writer studies literature, not the world. He lives in the world; he cannot miss it. . . . He is careful of what he reads, for that is what he will write. He is careful of what he learns, because that is what he will know" (68). Our developing writers live in the world as well and their lives are filled with experience, but it is the literature we link them to that helps them shape the potential for what writing can become. The vision they begin with will be shaped by all the texts they have read and heard and seen. That vision is a starting point, an igniter of sorts. The end product may or may not match the vision, but the vision gives shape to the developing ideas as the writer makes decisions about how to move from an entry in the notebook to a finished text. None of it is set in stone, but to envision requires premeditation. That's an interesting thought—premeditated writing. Don't we want our writers to meditate, reflect, daydream, and plan before launching on the journey?

Identify Cause

The writer confuses topic and vision.

Give the Writer Tools to Move Forward

- Use your notebook to show where you have made plans with attention to the focus of the text, the chunks or segments, how the text may begin and end, what format or genre you will write in.

- Sit with the writer to revisit a familiar text (perhaps a previous piece written by the student or you), and scaffold a conversation that leads the student to name the general topic of the story. Then help him recognize that the focus of the story comes from what the writer hopes to convey about that topic. Try this with a familiar mentor text as well.

Identify Cause

The writer is focused on a single scene and has not considered the text as a whole.

Give the Writer Tools to Move Forward

- Select a familiar text written by either you or the student. Focus on one scene (such as a scene where the tension is rising, or the scene where a significant detail or event is revealed), and imagine this is the entire text. Lead the writer to discover that the scene he is currently focused on is perhaps the most interesting part, so it naturally has his attention. Now the task is to bring the reader along to see what the writer has seen and know what he knows. Scaffold for the writer how to lead up to and away from that pivotal scene. Imagine with him how the text would begin to bring a reader into this scene. Imagine how it could end. Explore several options as you would if planning a vacation.

- Select a familiar text, and imagine what the author's vision may have been. Think backward with the writer to consider some of the decisions the author may have had to consider before and during the writing. Map out a plan that could have resulted in the finished text you are examining.

Mentor texts:
Home Run by Robert Burleigh
Roller Coaster by Marla Frazee
Enemy Pie by Derek Munson

Identify Cause

The writer has a sequence of events or a general plot, yet there is no clear theme tying it all together.

Give the Writer Tools to Move Forward

- Invite the writer to think aloud about the text and tell you what she is trying to develop. Take notes as she speaks. Now read back to her what she has said, and ask her to tell what she hopes her readers will think about or remember when they finish.

- Ask the writer to write a bumper sticker that tells what she hopes her text conveys to the reader. Using the bumper sticker as a lens, read her text. Ask her to listen as you read aloud. Pause after each segment to talk through how the text is (or isn't) building toward the bumper sticker.

- It may be helpful to simply be clear about your terms. Explain that plot is *what happens*, the sequence of events. But theme is a bigger message, a way of tying all those bits together to say something. Theme helps the writer focus and helps readers understand why we should care and why it matters to the reader and why it tugs at us for a response or an emotion.

- Ask the writer to make a list of what her story is about. Read the list together, and search for what those ideas may have in common. This may help bring some clarity to the writer's focus. Attempt to weave the list into a bumper sticker that can help focus a rewrite.

Identify Cause

The writer has given little thought to mentor texts as models.

Give the Writer Tools to Move Forward

- Ask the writer to select a potential idea from his notebook. Now host a conversation with the writer to model the questions one may consider when envisioning: What do I want the reader to know? (List facts, feelings, information, etc., or list a set of questions the reader should be able to answer after reading.) So where might I begin? (List three or four possible points of entry with attention to time of day or year, location, or point in the sequence of events.) End? (Review an anchor chart exploring possible ways of bringing closure to a text, and consider which of the several may best work for her intentions.) What ways could I move this text forward? (Pull a set of texts to examine possible text structures and text features for organizing the work.) What genre or format might work best? (Consider what she wants to create, and examine two to four options from a stack of mentor texts.) What have I read or seen that is like what I want to make?

- Using the focusing questions, ask the writer to think through these ideas in her notebook. She may choose to explore several options and perhaps even a couple of drafts after that before deciding how she wants to proceed.

Finding a Focus

4

Every day people buy a book, check out a DVD, talk and plan and convince themselves they can remodel a bathroom, build a deck, or landscape the backyard in a single Saturday afternoon. They make a list of tools and supplies and head off to purchase what they need with the very best intentions and perhaps with a clear vision of the outcome. What they lack is a clear understanding of what it will take to go from gathering supplies to realizing the vision. And no matter how explicit the directions in those books and DVDs, the lack of experience prevents them from conceiving the amount of skill and time each step will take. So they jump into the project with great enthusiasm and little more than a hazy notion of what lies ahead. It isn't until they are well into the mess that they realize the project that once seemed so easy, so sensible, and so manageable in the video is actually much larger and more complex than anything they could have imagined. We are imagining that most of you can relate to this experience. Maybe you have misjudged the scope of a project, took on more than you were prepared for, and abandoned one or more of these projects yourself. That would not be uncommon in the experience of an adult. The scope of a project is difficult for many of us to grasp, and even more so for anyone lacking experience.

Likewise, inexperienced writers easily step into the quicksand of good ideas and making big plans without having any real sense of the small details and the actual work it will take to execute the plan. In our experience this out-of-control feeling has roots in at least two sources: 1) inadequate knowledge of the topic, and 2) inadequate understanding of the parameters of the type of text.

Inexperienced writers often plateau here because they have only general knowledge of the topic and lack depth of understanding. In this instance the writer may be fueled by her intense interest in a topic and delve into the project without recognizing that her interest is not grounded in sufficient knowledge. This alone may result in sweeping generalizations and an inability to zero in on the specifics needed to support her assertions and offer elaboration that brings clarity to her writing. Or it may result in an inability to determine what is and isn't significant to support the reader's understanding. In either case it doesn't take long before the project that once seemed perfect becomes overwhelming and confusing.

A similar result occurs when the writer delves into a type of writing she is not grounded in. Taking on a new type of writing before exploring the territory as a reader is risky. The project can easily feel unwieldy and overwhelming when you do not have a grasp of the parameters of the text type. Writers need to spend time reading texts of the same type they plan to create with attention to the way those texts are organized, how ideas are developed and presented, how details are layered in to elaborate significant points and support assertions, and notice how text features are employed and why. Our work with mentor texts must delve as deeply into *why* as into *how* in writing. And our developing writers must be readers who are willing to explore the territory before they try to map it.

Identify Cause

The writer does not have a clear understanding of the scope of the project.

Give the Writer Tools to Move Forward

- Ask him to tell you what he plans to write (type of text), and find an example for him to examine closely. Scaffold his understanding of the scope of the text. Where does it begins and end? What is included? What did the author decide to exclude? Imagine how the text would have been different if the writer had made different decisions.

Mentor texts:
Roller Coaster by Marla Frazee
Home Run by Robert Burleigh
Underground by Shane W. Evans
Who Would Win? series by Jerry Pallotta

- Help him see the more narrow focus of an essay by comparing that to a feature article. Or compare the scope of a feature article with an all-about book.

Mentor texts:
Landry Jones by Pablo S. Borre
SIKids.com (feature article), *ABCs of Baseball* by Peter Golenbock (all-about book)

- Ask him to list essential questions he hopes to answer for his readers. Then make note of the information he has and make a list of the research he will need.

Identify Cause

The writer has an unwieldy collection of notes.

Give the Writer Tools to Move Forward

- Ask the writer to sort the notes into groups that will help her find an organizing framework. For a nonfiction project, that may be categories or headings. For a fiction project, it may be a plot map or chunks like beginning, middle, and end.

- Organize the notes, and assign a priority to each group. Decide what must be included and what could be left out.

- Return to the essential questions guiding the work. These questions can be sequenced in a way that may serve as an organizing framework. Once the framework has been determined an introduction can be drafted to set up the project. The essential questions or segments on the plot map can be used to guide the writer through manageable chunks.

Mentor texts:

Gather a small collection of texts by authors such as Gail Gibbons, Seymour Simon, Nicola Davies, Sneed Collard, or Melissa Stewart. Examine these for categories and structure to create a schema for organizing your notes.

4

Finding a Focus

Identify Cause

The writer is unable to narrow the focus of the project to find a manageable scope.

Give the Writer Tools to Move Forward

- Interview the writer about her topic and plan for the project. Ask what she has in mind. Once you've determined the type of text she is trying to make, assist her in gathering a small stack of examples. Examine the examples with attention to how much detail is included. If the text is fairly sophisticated, then either guide her toward a scene or segment within the example or assist her in finding a more manageable mentor text to explore.

- While exploring various examples, note the scope of each project. For example, the story doesn't take in all the details of a week at the beach. Rather, it focuses on a family gathering, collecting shells together, and having a cookout. Or the text doesn't take on everything there is to know about the loggerhead turtle but instead focuses on the night the turtles come ashore and lay their eggs. Help your writer grasp the concept of scope by noting what the mentor text *did* include and what the author *decided* to leave out.

Mentor texts:
The Boy Who Harnessed the Wind by William Kamkwamba and Bryan Mealer
Roller Coaster by Marla Frazee
A Storm Called Katrina by Myron Uhlberg

Identify Cause

The writer has too little experience with the type of writing he is attempting in this project.

Give the Writer Tools to Move Forward

- Collect a small stack of example texts of the type he plans to write. Examine the texts together, making note of common text features and attributes such as types of leads, use of headings, transitions between scenes or segments, use of details, the role of description, types of endings, the progression of information from start to finish, and the framework or organizing structure for the text. In a way you are creating a mental map for the territory of this type of writing.

- From this stack select a mentor text where the desired features and attributes are exemplars. "Interview" the text with the writer to determine what this text does that he wants to try out in his project.

- Develop a "map" of the text type that will help your writer get organized and develop a scheme for moving forward.

Identify Cause

The writer has keen interest but only general knowledge of the topic.

Give the Writer Tools to Move Forward

- Ask the writer to go to his notebook and make a list of what he believes is absolutely essential information for his project. Examine the list with him, and interview him about each point on the list. Make notes and help him see what he knows and where he may need to revisit his experience or do some research.

- Guide him to resources (his experience, photos, artifacts, articles, interviews, essays, stories, narratives, picture books, poems, or songs, depending on what he is planning to create). Use his passion for the topic to fuel further exploration and reading to build more specific knowledge and focus for the topic.

- Ask him to log his insights, questions, or notes in his notebook or on note cards. He may find it helpful to use headings such as "What I believe is true," "What I remember," "Questions," and "Notes" as he explores the topic further.

Identify Cause

The writer is inexperienced with the process of breaking down the project into small, manageable chunks.

Give the Writer Tools to Move Forward

- Using a mentor text as a framework, consider the chunks of the text. This could mean looking at the text as a series of scenes, creating a plot map, or moving forward category by category, following a logical chronology of events, or developing a list of places in the setting. Whichever organizing structure is selected to hold the project together can also help the writer see the scope of the project. This vision can also develop the text one chunk at a time.

Mentor texts:

All the Places to Love by Patricia MacLachlan
Bubba and Beau Meet the Relatives by Kathi Appelt
City Dog, Country Frog by Mo Willems
Crow Call by Lois Lowry
Saturdays and Teacakes by Lester L. Laminack

4

Finding a Focus

Identify Cause

The writer has keen interest and well developed knowledge of the topic. However, he cannot zero in on a specific aspect for this particular project.

Give the Writer Tools to Move Forward

- If the source of the writer's plateau has its roots in his intimate knowledge of the topic, it may also be true that he has a difficult time zooming in on a specific point that would be pertinent to someone who is much less informed about the topic. Show him examples of texts on a similar topic, and guide him to realize how the author chose to feature only an aspect of the topic.

- Interview the writer to find out both the range and depth of his knowledge and where his passion for the topic is focused. Makes notes as you listen, and show him several possible focal points for his project.

Developing a Lead

5

A lead, like a front porch, is the entry to the text. The lead welcomes the reader and invites him in. This "front porch" experience is charged with setting a tone, suggesting a focus, and helping the reader anticipate what may lie ahead—all this is in addition to the very important job of enticing him to continue reading.

Leads get a lot attention in the writing workshop. We have seen several minilessons devoted to developing leads. One suggestion we hear again and again is to "grab" or "hook" the reader in the opening lines. Clearly, we have no argument with the intention, but we prefer William Zinsser's (2001) more gentle term, "capture." Common sense and the advice of many writers suggest the best way to become better at writing leads is to read lots of them. But we must also be attentive to what those leads do to launch the piece and bring the reader in. We must study not only *how* it is done but also come to understand *why it is done that way* in this particular text if we

are to make the best use of knowing how. For us, the lead can capture the reader in many ways. It may be done with bold and startling statements or a clamor of sound effects, with engaging dialogue, through lush descriptions, or an overheard phone conversation, interior monologue, the introduction of a character, a robust sense of place, or any of a number of options. But let's also remember just as there are many purposes for writing, there are also purposes for leads. There are leads meant to grab you and others meant to seduce you. Some take you by the hand and walk you into the text, and some intentionally pull you so slowly into the flow of the language you never even realize that you are already captured. Leads can set the stage, launch the action, or introduce a character, a problem, or an issue. Leads can taunt you or prod you or lure you. Leads can do the writer's bidding if she is clear, focused, and informed.

The leads of some less experienced writers fall flat and leave the reader uninterested in reading further. And some overfocus on the opening to the point that the lead outweighs the remainder of the text, making it feel top heavy. In either instance the reader is likely to be overwhelmed or confused. Many experienced writers spend a great deal of time developing the lead because it sets the stage for all that follows. Donald Murray (1990) wrote, "I often have to write many first lines—twenty-five, fifty, seventy-five. I used to have my students write at least fifteen or twenty first lines for a piece of writing. It is not time wasted; in fact it makes the writing go faster because the writing has found its voice, its aim, its destination before the writer has written a paragraph, and many of the problems that would have been revealed in a draft are foreseen, avoided, or solved" (119).

So let's move forward and explore what may lie underneath a writer's struggle with getting the lead just right. And let's explore how we may nudge the writer onward in developing competence, confidence, and control.

Identify Cause

The writer is unclear of the purpose of the lead.

Give the Writer Tools to Move Forward

- Revisit a familiar text, and focus on the lead. Note with the student what the lead is doing in the text—that is, what "job" does the lead do for the reader in the making of meaning? Link that insight to having the writer talk about the "job" he wants the lead to do in this text.

Mentor texts:

Enemy Pie by Derek Munson—establishes the setting and poses a problem to entice the reader

Twilight Comes Twice by Ralph Fletcher—establishes a specific time of day, sets a tone for the text, provides framework for the contrast, and entices the reader to come along

Identify Cause

The writer over relies on "stock" opening lines (such as "once upon a time," "one time," or "long ago").

Give the Writer Tools to Move Forward

- Have the writer tell you the focus of the text (for example, the character, the event, the location, a passionate opinion, or a plea for action). Revisit the lead as written, and talk about what that lead suggests to the reader. Ask the writer to consider what she hopes for in the lead, and recast the opening words.

Mentor texts:

A Sick Day for Amos McGee by Phillip C. Stead—introduces the main character and gives insight to his habits

No One But You by Douglas Wood—states the premise of the text, gives focus to the theme

Identify Cause

The writer has placed more emphasis on "grabbing" or "hooking" the reader than on connecting to the text to set the stage.

Give the Writer Tools to Move Forward

- Read the lead aloud, and ask the writer what it suggests or where it makes the reader think the text is going. Does this match the vision for the text?

Mentor texts:

Dream Weaver by Jonathan London—draws attention to being observant and present, to being focused

Farmer Duck by Martin Waddell—introduces the main character, and states the problem he must overcome

Identify Cause

The writer has no clear vision for focus of the text.

Give the Writer Tools to Move Forward

- Link back to a familiar text, read the lead aloud, and remind the writer of the message of the text. Demonstrate how the lead helps take you into the essence of the text.

Mentor texts:

A Nation's Hope: The Story of Boxing Legend Joe Lewis by Matt de la Pena—concise, clear, and direct statement of date and location, sets the situation, and builds tension that will take you into the text

Soar, Elinor! by Tami Lewis Brown—offers a contextual reference, and sets up a contrast that reveals essential traits of the main character

Developing a Lead

Identify Cause

The writer has placed too great an emphasis on developing the lead in isolation, removed from its role within the context of the text as a whole, resulting in a top-heavy opening, an underdeveloped body, and a weak ending.

Give the Writer Tools to Move Forward

- Fold a sheet of paper into three segments so that the top and bottom segments make up only a small portion, perhaps one-quarter of the page each, leaving approximately half of the page for the center segment. Use the segments to demonstrate the relationship that should exist between the lead, the body of the text, and the ending.

Opportunities for Study/Mentor Texts: Leads and the Work They Do in the Writing

The opportunity here is to explore leads with attention focused on the *work* the lead is doing in the text. We've listed several for you, hoping that from this list you'll be able to locate a small subset to explore in your classroom. Begin with a few titles, and present them as a read-aloud experience. Share each title two or three times before delving into specific aspects of any book.

As familiarity is gained, lead a discussion about the essence of the book, what it's about, and what they take from it. Return to the opening lines—the front porch—and note how those lines create a welcome or an invitation of sorts.

Now invite them to work together with favorite titles they select from independent reading, read-aloud experiences, guided reading, or book clubs. Repeat the process, and note the work being done by the lead in each of those books. The collective result may be a chart like the one below that can serve as a reminder of the work a lead can do when the writer is aware.

Leads: *Examples from Professional Writers*			
AUTHOR	TITLE	EXAMPLES FROM TEXT	WHAT IT DOES
Ruth Brown	*Gracie the Lighthouse Cat*	*Outside the storm was raging, but inside the lighthouse, Gracie and her kitten were warm and snug in the cozy parlor.*	Begins with a contrast of weather outside and inside, creating an emotional tone with the setting.
Tami Lewis Brown	*Soar, Elinor!*	*In 1917, some girls dressed their dolls. They played hopscotch, jump rope and jacks. But one little girl wanted more. Elinor Smith wanted to soar!*	Establishes a contextual frame (time, behavior, longing) for the main character.

(continues)

Leads: *Examples from Professional Writers (continued)*

AUTHOR	TITLE	EXAMPLES FROM TEXT	WHAT IT DOES
Donald Crews	*Bigmama's*	*Did you see her? Did you see Big Mama?*	Opens with questions speaking directly to the reader as if he or she is part of the story.
Donald Crews	*Shortcut*	*We looked . . . We listened . . . We decided to take the shortcut home. We should have taken the road.*	Opens with brief sentences, uses parallel language, creates tension, piques interest, and foreshadows events of the text.
Carolyn Crimi	*Henry & the Crazed Chicken Pirates*	*Henry and the Buccaneer Bunnies lived on an island. They spent their days reading books they had collected over the years, shooting one another out of cannons, and swinging from the masts of their ship. They were a happy bunch.*	Names the main characters, contextualizes them in a place, gives some sense of their routine, and provides a backdrop against which the tension can mount as the problem develops.
Matt de la Pena	*A Nation's Hope: The Story of Boxing Legend Joe Louis*	*Yankee Stadium, 1938. Packed crowd buzzing and bets bantered back and forth. The Bronx night air thick with summer.*	Establishes a contextual frame including place, time frame, and emotional tone.
Ralph Fletcher	*Twilight Comes Twice*	*Twice each day a crack opens between night and day. Twice twilight slips through that crack. It stays only a short time while night and day stand whispering secrets before they go their separate ways.*	Establishes a specific time of day, sets a tone for the text, provides framework for the contrast, and entices the reader to come along.

AUTHOR	TITLE	EXAMPLES FROM TEXT	WHAT IT DOES
Libba Moore Gray	*My Mama Had a Dancing Heart*	*My mama had a dancing heart and she shared that heart with me.*	Restates the title and establishes a connection between the narrator and the main character.
Jan Greenberg and Sandra Jordan	*Ballet for Martha*	*The dancer and choreographer. The composer. The artist. Together they created a ballet about a new home, a new family, a new life. A dance about America.*	Contains short sentence fragments.
Robie Harris	*The Day Leo Said I Hate You!*	*Today, Leo's mommy couldn't stop saying "No!"*	Sets tone and introduces a main character and a problem.
James Howe	*Brontorina*	*Brontorina had a dream.*	States the theme of the story.
G. Brian Karas	*Atlantic*	*I am the Atlantic Ocean.*	Contains personification and a straightforward declaration and identifies the narrator.
Jonathan London	*Dream Weaver*	*Nestled in the soft earth beside the path, you see a little yellow spider.*	Introduces the setting and character.
Loren Long	*Otis*	*There was once a friendly little tractor. His name was Otis, and every day Otis and his farmer worked together taking care of the farm they called home.*	Introduces the character.

(continues)

Leads: *Examples from Professional Writers (continued)*

AUTHOR	TITLE	EXAMPLES FROM TEXT	WHAT IT DOES
David McKee	*Elmer and the Rainbow*	*Elmer, the patchwork elephant, was in a cave, sheltering from a storm.*	Names the main character, and establishes place, including the weather conditions.
Pat Mora	*Book Fiesta!*	*Hooray! Today is our day.* *(Spanish sentence)* *Let's have fun today reading our favorite books.*	Begins with a declaration that sets the focus.
Derek Munson	*Enemy Pie*	*It should have been a perfect summer. My dad helped me build a tree house in our backyard. My sister was at camp for three whole weeks. And I was on the best baseball team in town. It should have been a perfect summer. But it wasn't.*	Entices the reader into wondering what went wrong.
Barack Obama	*Of Thee I Sing*	*Have I told you lately how wonderful you are? How the sound of your feet running from afar brings dancing rhythms to my day? How your laugh and sunshine spills into the room?*	Opens with questions from the narrator, and sets a tone for the text.
Lee Posey	*Night Rabbits*	*"Oh no, Elizabeth. The rabbits are eating my new lawn," my father says one morning at breakfast.*	Opens with dialogue.

AUTHOR	TITLE	EXAMPLES FROM TEXT	WHAT IT DOES
Doreen Rappaport	*Jack's Path of Courage*	*John F. Kennedy, called Jack by family and friends, was the second oldest of four boys and five girls in a wealthy, close-knit family.*	Names and introduces the main character by placing him in a family context.
Cynthia Rylant	*Night in the Country*	*There is no night so dark, so black as night in the country.*	Establishes the setting locale and time of day, creates a tone, and contrasts life inside and outside.
Charles R. Smith, Jr.	*Twelve Rounds to Glory*	*Bathed in beautiful light from parental love, brown skin shimmers with a glow from above. In 1942, the seventeenth of January, you entered the world in Louisville, Kentucky. Whites Only stores and Whites Only parks sifted you out because you were dark.*	Begins with rhyming language, and provides a context for the featured character.
Mark Sperring	*The Sunflower Sword*	*Once there was a land filled with fire and smoke and . . .*	Establishes the genre as a fairy tale.
Philip C. Stead	*A Sick Day for Amos McGee*	*Amos McGee was an early riser. Every morning when the alarm clock clanged, he swung his legs out of bed and swapped his pajamas for a fresh-pressed uniform.*	Names and introduces the main character.

(continues)

5

Developing a Lead

Leads: *Examples from Professional Writers (continued)*

AUTHOR	TITLE	EXAMPLES FROM TEXT	WHAT IT DOES
Matt Tavares	*Mudball*	*One fateful spring day in 1903, Little Andy Oyler practiced his swing—and tried not to listen to the heckling fans of the opposing team, the St. Paul Saints.*	Creates an ominous tone, and reveals specific traits of the character.
Martin Waddell	*Farmer Duck*	*There once was a duck who had the bad luck to live with a lazy old farmer. The duck did the work. The farmer stayed all day in bed.*	Identifies the main character, and establishes a situation for his story.
Martin Waddell	*Owl Babies*	*Once there were three baby owls: Sarah and Percy and Bill. They lived in a hole in the trunk of a tree with their Owl Mother.*	Introduces characters, and contextualizes them in a place.
Neil Waldman	*A Land of Big Dreamers*	*We hold these truths to be self-evident, that all men are created equal . . .*	Opens with a historical reference.
David Wiesner	*Art & Max*	*Careful Max!* *Hey, Art, that's great!*	Uses font and dialog to introduce the two main characters.
Douglas Wood	*A Quiet Place*	*Sometimes a person needs a quiet place. A place to rest your ears from bells ringing and whistles shrieking and grown-ups talking . . .*	Defines and establishes a personal preference or desire.

Leads: *Examples from Professional Writers (continued)*

AUTHOR	TITLE	EXAMPLES FROM TEXT	WHAT IT DOES
Douglas Wood	*No One But You*	*There are so many things in the world, so many important things to be taught, to be shown. But the best things, the most important ones of all, are the ones no one can teach you or show you or explain. No one can discover them but you!*	States the premise of the text.
Jane Yolen	*Grandad Bill's Song*	*Grandma, what did you do on the day Grandad died? I sat in my porch rocker, child, and I cried. I looked at the ocean all covered with foam and thought of my handsome young sailor gone home.*	Opens with question and answer between the two main characters.

Establishing a Context or Setting

6

Less experienced writers may think of setting as little more than "where it happens." Some will not think to let readers know that much. Dorothy Allison (2009) says, "[p]lace is often something you don't see because you're so familiar with it that you devalue it or dismiss it or ignore it. But in fact it is the information your reader most wants to know. . . . Your reader comes into your narrative to steal knowledge—who you are and what is all around you, what you use, or don't use, what you need, or fear, or want—all that sweet reverberating detail . . ." (7).

A well-crafted text situates the reader in the locale, builds a feeling within the situation, and establishes the tone and mood of the scene. Setting establishes a sense of place and helps the reader create parameters in which the characters and events exist. In this case, place is more than the geographic location on the GPS. Dorothy Allison contends that *place* is visual detail and requires context. "Place is where the 'I' goes. Place is what that

'I' looks at, what it doesn't look at. Is it happy? Is it sad? Is it afraid? Is it curious? . . . Place is not just a landscape—a list of flora and fauna and street names. . . . Place is feeling, and feeling is something a character expresses. . . . I want a story that is happening in a real place, which means a place that has meaning and that evokes emotions in the person who is telling me the story. Place is emotion . . ." (8–9).

Setting is an essential aspect of writing that provides the narrator and the characters and the events with a context, a framework within which to exist. Setting helps establish the atmosphere for emotions and feelings to rise. At times the setting is merely a required backdrop against which the action or events are played out—a stage if you will. Yet, there are other times when the setting is an essential part of the story itself. Some contend that setting can almost be a character. If, for example, your writer is working on a story about playing catch with a friend, it *could* happen almost anywhere there is ample space (park, school playground, ball field, vacant lot, or backyard). However, if an essential part of the story is a broken window on the neighbor's front porch, her reaction to that broken window, and the narrator's feelings of guilt and attempts for redemption, the setting, then, becomes an important part of the text itself. Less experienced writers may get caught up in the action and focus their writing energy on capturing sequential events or facts with no awareness of how setting influences those details. For example, the broken window may take on more significance on a clear, cold winter afternoon than a mild spring morning.

Consider the differences in the tone and mood of language that would be generated by a hour in a major league baseball stadium, an afternoon hike along a trail in fall, a rainy day spent alone in your room, an evening of fireworks downtown in a city, or five hours trapped in a blizzard on the interstate in a car with your family. And how would each of these stories shift if set in 1960 versus 2013? We want our students to have the ability to capture the energy of the place and the situation. As you read aloud to children, lead guided reading groups, or confer with individual readers, lead them to notice the role of the setting. Help them to see how the physical and emotional setting actually influences the tone of the language of the characters and of the narrator. And help them notice how these details assist the reader in constructing a more robust sense of what is happening.

Identify Cause

The writer assumes his readers know what he knows and sees the world as he does.

Give the Writer Tools to Move Forward

- Read the text aloud to the writer once through without stopping. Now read it a second time, and pause to ask relevant questions that highlight how a sense of place could clarify the text: So where were you when this part happens? Was it cold? Tell me about the weather that day? How did that make a difference in what you decided to do there? How were you feeling when that happened? What was going on around you? Does the place feel creepy? Exciting? Why?

Mentor texts:

Crow Call by Lois Lowry—takes you into the time, locale, and weather

Saturdays and Teacakes by Lester L. Laminack—the opening reveals a specific time and takes you along with the narrator as he bikes across town

Fireflies by Julie Brinckloe—the story provides explicit setting and tone throughout the book with carefully selected words that show a slower pace of life

Identify Cause

The writer is more focused on sequencing details, including facts and getting the ideas down.

Give the Writer Tools to Move Forward

- Remember the influence of our reading lives upon our writing lives. If the reading life has focused on accumulating facts and details to give back in assessment, it is possible that the student has developed the habit of reading for detail without thinking about the relationships between action and setting. As a reader he may not recognize the layers of meaning or even consider how place and time and atmosphere has influenced the thoughts and actions of characters. That could be reflected in what he produces as a writer.

- Return to a familiar text where the setting or sense of place is fleshed out and viable to the writing. Read it along with the writer, pausing to think aloud about the way the author has woven place into the text, which helps you (as reader) make sense of it.

Mentor texts:

Appalachia: Voices of Sleeping Birds by Cynthia Rylant—setting is essential in this text and is revealed through the physical description of the geography, flora, and fauna

All the Places to Love by Patricia MacLachlan—the opening lines take us back in time to a quiet, rural existence where land and place were valued

Identify Cause

The writer has an undeveloped sense of the power of setting to contribute to the tone, mood, and contextual framework of the story.

Give the Writer Tools to Move Forward

- Select a nonfiction text and read the opening segments. Note how the attention to setting provides a context for all the information about polar bears.

- Contrast the contextual frame of two very different texts.

Mentor texts:
Polar Bears by Gail Gibbons versus *Red Wolf Country* by Jonathan London, or *Owl Moon* by Jane Yolen versus *The Barn Owls* by Tony Johnston

Note how these contrasts of setting help to demonstrate the importance not only of physical place but also of weather and climatic conditions and the influence of habitat upon action.

Opportunities for Study/Mentor Texts: Exploring Where It Happens and Why That's Important

The opportunity for study here is to explore a collection of texts, including both fiction and nonfiction, with attention targeted to the importance of place as more than the physical location. The idea here is twofold. First we want to develop the idea that place matters; it helps the reader to situate events, characters, or information. And, second, we want to broaden the understanding of place to include more than the physical geography of location.

Following a procedure very similar to the opportunity for study with leads, first read a few of these titles aloud two or three times each over several days. As the group develops familiarity with the text and has a sense of the whole, move into a close reading of those parts where the writer makes place an important aspect of the whole. In each case note how the writing helps us, as readers, build not only an understanding of *where* it happens but also a sense of *how that matters*. In essence, we are teaching *function* before *form*; that is, we are trying to teach the *why* and *when* before teaching them *how*.

Now select another set of familiar texts, and invite your students to read them with an eye for where the writers feature place and how that matters to the reader's understanding. Open these insights to discussion, and create a list of generalizations regarding the importance of place in our writing.

Examples from Professional Writers That Show How the Setting Is Established			
AUTHOR	TITLE	EXAMPLE FROM TEXT	WHAT IT DOES
Gail Gibbons	*Polar Bears*	1) *The snow blows, the wind howls. The temperature is very cold, hovering around –30 degrees Fahrenheit (–34 degrees Celsius) . . .*	1) Immediately establishes a climate that is vastly different from what most readers will know.
		2) *The polar bear lives in the Arctic, the area that surrounds the North Pole . . .*	2) Places the featured subject in a specific geographic location.

(continues)

AUTHOR	TITLE	EXAMPLE FROM TEXT	WHAT IT DOES
Tony Johnston	*The Barn Owls*	The barn has stood in the wheat field one hundred years at least. Owls have slept there all day long and dozed in the scent of wheat.	Provides a contextual framework in time and location.

Lester L. Laminack	*Saturdays and Teacakes*	1) Every Saturday I coasted down our long steep drive, slowing only enough to make the turn onto Thompson Street, . . . and on up to Chandler's Phillips 66.
		   That's where I crossed the highway that ran right through the center of our town.
		2) In our little town everyone knew everybody . . . and told everything to anyone who would listen. So I always looked both ways.
		3) This was where my tires gave up the humming of pavement and began the crunching of gravel. . . . I slammed on my brakes, sending a shower of tiny pebbles into her flowers.
		4) Every Saturday Mammaw was there, sitting on her old metal glider—criiick-craaack-criiick-craaack—sipping a cup of Red Diamond Coffee and waiting. She was waiting for me. No one else. Just me.
		   Every Saturday she had hot biscuits, sweet butter, and Golden Eagle Syrup waiting on the kitchen table.
		5) In Mammaw's big kitchen, . . . pooling up on the checkerboard floor.
			1) Suggests a distance to travel, and contrasts small town and suburban neighborhoods.
			2) Creates a sense of knowing and being known, a sense of confidence and safety. Helps to place the narrator in a family context.
			3) Contrasts the paved road and gravel drive, again supporting the notion of a small, rural town.
			4) Sets an easy, relaxed patience with her actions. The specific brand names help set a regional feel.
			5) Zooming in on the kitchen "spotlights" this place as one of significance.

AUTHOR	TITLE	EXAMPLE FROM TEXT	WHAT IT DOES
Jonathan London	*Red Wolf Country*	1) *Two red wolves roam the coastal wetlands. A rare snow has fallen, and icicles glitter in the sweet gum and loblolly pine.* 2) *With her mate, she climbs a low rise, and as the sun sinks into clouds of gold and silk, the coats of the two wolves flare up like bright red flames.* 3) *There below, downwind in a frozen marsh, a small dark animal ambles along in the moonlit southern night.* *The red wolves step delicately through the soft snow. Gracefully, they drift down toward the shining pond and press themselves flat.*	1) Suggests a region, and notes an atypical climatic condition that will serve as a contrast for the featured subject. 2) Shows how the wolf, normally less visible in the "typical" climatic conditions, becomes a stark contrast here. 3) Describes the climatic conditions (the snow and the implied bright moonlight) that allow us to view what may typically go unnoticed, thus serving as a "spotlight" of sorts.
Lois Lowry	*Crow Call*	1) *It's morning, early, barely light, cold for November.* 2) *We eat quickly, watching the sun rise across the Pennsylvania farmlands.* 3) *Grass, frozen after its summer softness, crunches under our feet; the air is sharp and supremely clear, free from the floating pollens of summer . . .* 4) *It's quieter than summer. There are no animal sounds, no bird-waking noises . . . waiting for the wind that will free them. Our breath is steam.*	1) Establishes the time of day and season of the year. 2) Establishes the geographic location. 3) Establishes a feel for the place and the conditions. 4) Gives a sense of the cold, the sound, and the feeling as well as a visual.

(continues)

6

Examples from Professional Writers That Show How the Setting Is Established (continued)

AUTHOR	TITLE	EXAMPLE FROM TEXT	WHAT IT DOES
Patricia MacLachlan	*All the Places to Love*	1) *On the day I was born my grandmother wrapped me in a blanket made from the wool of her sheep. She held me up in the open window . . .* 2) *Through the meadows and hay field, the cows watched us and the sheep scattered . . .* *We jumped from rock to rock, across the river to where the woods began, where bunchberry grew under the pine-needle path and trillium bloomed . . .*	1) Suggests a time decades ago because in these first few sentences we surmise the narrator was born at home. 2) The remaining description clearly suggests a rural, bucolic location and a supportive and loving emotional setting. It is clear that place is an essential component to the lives of these characters, as even the title suggests.
Patricia MacLachlan	*What You Know First*	1) *I won't go, I'll say, to a new house, to the new place, to a land I've never seen.* 2) *He doesn't know about the slough where the pipits feed. Where the geese sky-talk in the spring. That baby hasn't even seen winter with snow drifting hard against fences . . .* 3) *And I'll try hard to remember the songs, and the sound of the rooster at dawn, and how soft the cows' ears are when you touch them, so the baby will know what he knew first.*	1) Suggests a strong reluctance to leave, a clinging to the known. 2) Establishes the contrast of reasons not to move. 3) Suggests the new location will be a contrast to this way of life, making the need to cling to memories and old ways more poignant.

AUTHOR	TITLE	EXAMPLE FROM TEXT	WHAT IT DOES
Derek Munson	*Enemy Pie*	*It should have been a perfect summer. My dad helped me build a tree house in our backyard. My sister was at camp for three whole weeks. And I was on the best baseball team in town. It should have been a perfect summer. But it wasn't.*	Builds tension, and sets a tone that something went wrong. The details suggest a neighborhood with large trees, perhaps a small town or suburban neighborhood. Frames a context for what is to come.
Cynthia Rylant	*Appalachia: The Voices of Sleeping Birds*	*1) In a certain part of the country called Appalachia you will find dogs named Prince or King living in little towns with names like Coal City and Sally's Backbone . . . against the hill roads they call hollows.* *2) The owners of these dogs who live in Appalachia . . . Many of them were born in coal camps in tiny houses which stood on poles and on the sides of which you could draw a face with your finger because coal dust had settled on their walls like snow. The owners of these dogs grew up more used to trees than sky . . . They weren't sure about going beyond these mountains, going until the land becomes flat or ocean, and so they stayed . . . sun would come up in the morning and set again at night.*	1) Pairs specific geography with a feeling for cultural differences. 2) Extends the setting with a close-up view of homes, creating a context for the people we will likely meet here, the lives they live, and how their existence may be similar to or different from what we know.

(continues)

6

Establishing a Context or Setting

AUTHOR	TITLE	EXAMPLE FROM TEXT	WHAT IT DOES
Jane Yolen	*Owl Moon*	*It was late one winter night, long past my bedtime, when Pa and I went owling. There was no wind. The trees stood still as giant statues. And the moon was so bright the sky seemed to shine. Somewhere behind us a train whistle blew, long and low, like a sad, sad song.*	Immediately takes the reader into the time of day and builds a sense of wonder. The details about weather and the moon and the contrast of silence and the train whistle create a quiet tone and sense of something special.

Wandering Off on a Tangent

Perhaps you have been in the middle of telling a story when a detail captured your attention and you found yourself saying, "Oh, that makes me think of . . ." and off you went. Before you knew it, you had lost your focus and couldn't remember where you were heading before going off on that "bird walk." Maybe we chuckle and blame it on age. Or we laugh and say, "Oh, what were we talking about?"

So we shouldn't find it surprising that developing writers sometimes find themselves captivated by a random thought spinning off from a detail they have just laid down in print. It certainly isn't news that the attention of a young person can bounce in unexpected directions like a Ping-Pong ball (and that includes when they are writing). When a detail or line of thought or a side story related to the topic captivates a less experienced writer, his mind will veer off course, and, well, the pencil just follows. What we fail to acknowledge in these situations is

that the writer is busily engaged in capturing these rogue thoughts on paper. If you point out the shift in his focus on the page, the young writer may appear incredulous. In the child's mind his text likely makes perfect sense. And to further complicate things, the "bird walk" may be well written and engaging, just off focus and therefore distracting and confusing for a reader.

Be gentle. Be patient. Do not rush. Let him know writing is a process that often unfolds slowly. Make it clear that it is not unusual for a writer to work through several rewrites before getting a clear focus. In fact, one of the tangents taken in an early draft may actually develop as the main focus of the next rewrite. Perhaps these "bird walk" tangents can be repurposed in an idea file or pasted into the writer's notebook for future exploration. Kaye Gibbons keeps a file on her computer for "decent outtakes" where she places chunks of text that do not work in her current novel but may have value in a future work. We can lead our developing writers to do the same.

Or perhaps you recall Anne Lamott's story of the time her brother had procrastinated for over three months avoiding a report on birds. Finally the day came when the report was due the following morning. Her brother was feeling overwhelmed by the enormity of the project. Their father's response was, "Bird by bird, buddy. Just take it bird by bird" (1994, 19). What works in this advice is twofold. First it divides up the task into manageable chunks. That alone helps to reduce the enormity of the project. And more to the point at hand, the advice provides an organizing principle right from the start. Having a clearly defined framework helps the writer remain focused with purpose and intention.

Having a frame of reference (such as a plot map, a list of significant events or details, or a "bumper sticker" or theme) can help the writer pause along the way to ensure the journey is following the path of his intentions. Of course, this assumes the writer is clear about his intentions from the outset. For some, meandering along the way through a first draft may be necessary to find *the* focus. Inexperienced writers may need to be nudged to continue asking themselves: What do I really want to say? What do I want the reader to leave with? What questions do I need to answer for the reader? Is this building toward the meaning I am trying to construct with the reader?

7

Wandering Off on a Tangent

Identify Cause

The writer does not differentiate between relevant and distracting details.

 ## *Give the Writer Tools to Move Forward*

- Choose a familiar mentor text to read together. As you read along, list details that are laid down. Attend to the text as it unfolds, and make note of how a detail from early in the text is connected to information revealed further in. Demonstrate how a significant detail can focus the reader's attention and help connect information from one part of the text to another.

Mentor text:
Enemy Pie by Derek Munson

- Using the same familiar mentor text, select a scene and rewrite in the air (read/tell the text), adding in extraneous details the writer did not include (but may have known). Talk with the writer about how those extra details may have been "accurate" but would not have helped the reader remain connected and focused.

Mentor texts:
The Snowy Day by Ezra Jack Keats
Bigmama's by Donald Crews

Identify Cause

The writer does not have a clearly defined focus.

Give the Writer Tools to Move Forward

- If there is a vision in place, then revisit the vision and note the intended focus. Read the piece to the writer as he listens for a spot (or spots) where the focus shifts. Invite him to bracket those spots in the text. Reread the piece, leaving out the bracketed segments. Ask the reader to talk through what he notices.

- Remind him that these bracketed segments can be placed in a revision file. Any one of them may be useful in another text.

- Review each bracketed segment, asking the writer to talk about why he considered that bit to be important. Attempt to understand the logic he is using for making decisions about what is and isn't a significant detail.

- Interview the writer to determine if the focus of the piece may lie in one of the "bird walk" segments. Perhaps one of the segments may need to be developed as an independent text.

- If it is clear that the writer is still exploring the topic, then return to "Exploring a Topic" and follow the suggestions there.

Mentor texts:
Pigs by Gail Gibbons
Mud by Mary Lyn Ray
Bigmama's by Donald Crews
Miss Rumphius by Barbara Cooney
Dave the Potter by Laban Carrick Hill

Identify Cause

The writer doesn't understand the need to reread with the vision in mind.

Give the Writer Tools to Move Forward

- Create a plot line, list of events, table of contents, outline, or some other visual to help the writer see what is included in the writing. Compare that to the intentions laid out in the vision, and note the distracters. Revise accordingly.

- Ask the writer to turn to a clean page in her notebook and write a bumper sticker that captures what she is trying to say in the text. Have her listen as you read her draft aloud to her. Ask her to list things that go with her bumper sticker.

- Ask the writer to make a list of three or four statements telling what she thinks the text is about. Jot those down in your notes. This will give you a sense of her intentions or reveal that she isn't really clear about her focus yet. Ask her to read the piece aloud to you as you make notes regarding where her text contributes to or detracts from her purpose statements. As she reaches the end, help her think through whether she has greater emphasis on one statement over another. This may help clarify her focus and may help weed out distraction.

Mentor texts:
Henry's Freedom Box by Ellen Levine
The Boy Who Harnessed the Wind by William Kamkwamba and Bryan Mealer
Born and Bred in the Great Depression by Jonah Winter
Saturdays and Teacakes by Lester L. Laminack

Identify Cause

The writer has lost focus and can't seem to regain her bearings.

Give the Writer Tools to Move Forward

- Instruction in reading has overfocused on making connections and has led the reader away from the author's purpose for the text.

- Invite the writer to put the text aside for a day and read a stack of texts that are similar (topic, structure, style, and so on) to what she has envisioned. After reading each text write a brief bumper sticker. Note how that statement captures the focus of the text. The next morning you may say something like, "Now think about what you read and how those writers stay focused on the same topic from start to finish. Let's return to your text. Before we read it together let's write a bumper sticker for what you want to do here. You hold the bumper sticker, and I'll read your writing aloud. Stop me if you notice the focus changing."

- Talk with the writer and explain that writers sometimes need a bit of distance (physical and emotional) from their texts in order to move forward. Suggest that she take a day and move into her notebook to explore a bit. If, for example, she has been writing a persuasive essay, she may try writing a few poems or a letter to express her thoughts on the topic. Working with the topic in a new form may help her to find a bit of clarity on the topic and determine what is most important to her.

- Ask the writer to write a bumper sticker for her intentions with this text. Read the text aloud as the writer listens with the bumper sticker in front of her. Pause after each segment, and talk with the writer to decide together what that segment is about. Post that statement on a sticky note. Make note of any place where the text moves away from the intended bumper sticker.

Controlling Details

8

As less experienced writers begin getting thoughts on paper we often attempt to extend their texts by prompting them to "add some details." This suggestion, without specific guidance regarding *where* and *why the details matter* may result in a hyperfocus on description that pulls the writer away from his intentions. In that case the writer, doing what he thinks we are suggesting, may get so caught up in layering in details that he loses perspective and finds himself lost in his own work. Many of us have seen developing writers get caught up in trying to describe everything with lavish physical detail that overpowers the purpose of the text they are writing. It's as if they have come to believe detail trumps meaning, story, or message.

You've heard the saying, "He can't see the forest for the trees." It's that sort of notion. The writer may become so focused on specificity that he loses sight of why those details matter to the development of the text he is writing.

In those situations, the writer finds it difficult to distinguish between relevant details and extraneous ones. The result may be a richly detailed text that a *reader* finds incredibly difficult to navigate. This plateau in writing is, of course, instructionally induced. Children learn what our actions and behaviors teach far more readily than what is written in our plans.

So let's be clear in our teaching. There is a significant distinction between "add some details" and teaching developing writers about the importance of detail to bring specificity to their writing. Clearly details matter, but only when those details have work to do in a text. Understanding what that work is can make the writing more precise and focused and, more important, hone the writer's skill in crafting a text. Our challenge in teaching, then, becomes leading writers to understand that "writing becomes more beautiful when it becomes specific" (Fletcher 1993, 48) and that "[c]oncrete details allow the writer to *understate* an important truth rather than clubbing the reader over the head with it. Such details have an almost magical way of getting to the heart of the complex issues, making explanations unnecessary" (49, 51). To do this we must help developing writers recognize relevant details in their reading and help them understand the importance of those details to their construction of meaning. Lead the writer to notice where details open the text and move it forward. Explore not only *how* it was done but also *why* it makes a difference in that specific place in the text. "When details of character and setting appeal to the senses, they create an experience for the reader that leads to understanding. When we say 'I see,' we most often mean 'I understand.' Inexperienced writers may choose the obvious detail, the man puffing on the cigarette, the young woman chewing on what's left of her fingernails.

Those details fail to tell—unless the man is dying of lung cancer or the woman is anorexic" (Clark 2011, 72). In short, relevant details shine a light on what is important. They draw the reader's attention toward what matters most in the construction of meaning. As teachers we must help them develop the ability to recognize what is significant in their reading lives to enable them as writers to have the ability to spotlight what is significant with detail and specificity. As teachers we have work to do in reading as well as in writing on this issue.

Identify Cause

Instruction has focused on the need to "add some details" without adequate emphasis on why those details matter.

Give the Writer Tools to Move Forward

- Remind the writer that writers never waste details, so the details have work to do. Read through the text with the writer, noting how each detail "works." Make note of details that aren't "working" (contributing to the development of the text), and consider revision.

- Select a familiar book and conduct a quick "detail audit" with the writer. Make note of details that are laid down in the text, and note how each one of them contributes to the development of the text. Lead the writer to notice that there are no "stray" details.

Mentor texts:
Enemy Pie by Derek Munson
The Boy Who Harnessed the Wind by William Kamkwamba and Bryan Mealer
Henry's Freedom Box by Ellen Levine
Saturdays and Teacakes by Lester L. Laminack
Crow Call by Lois Lowry

Identify Cause

The writer overgeneralizes the need for specificity.

Give the Writer Tools to Move Forward

- Put the writer's text aside for a moment. Have the writer list the most important parts that she believes a reader must know to get her intentions. Jot down the list as she speaks. Return to the text, and place a star next to segments where this information is presented. Revisit the text, and note where details in other places may be diverting the reader's attention away from the writer's intentions.

Mentor texts:
Penguins by Seymour Simon
Wolves by Gail Gibbons
ABC's of Baseball by Peter Golenbock
Who Would Win? series by Jerry Pallotta

Identify Cause

The writer may find details and descriptions "easy" to write but doesn't understand the purpose of including details in writing.

Give the Writer Tools to Move Forward

- Ask the writer to read his text aloud as you make note of the details he has included. When he has reached the end, pause for a moment. Then comment on how well he develops detail. Read a few examples of relevant details back to him. Now ask him why writers have details in a text. Listen to his thinking, and try to gain insight into his understanding of the role of detail in writing. Now read a segment from your own writing (or from a familiar published text) where detail is used effectively. Point out how the narrative around that segment simply moves the text forward without the degree of specificity found in the detailed segment. Discuss how detail helps the reader know what is and isn't most important.

Mentor texts:
Jamaica's Find by Juanita Havill
Jake's 100th Day of School by Lester L. Laminack
The Other Side by Jacqueline Woodson
Miss Tizzy by Libba Moore Gray

Identify Cause

The writer may believe details and description are "valued" by the teacher.

Give the Writer Tools to Move Forward

- Clarify your intentions. You may find it helpful to note how well the writer has developed the ability to write detail. Make sure she understands how pleased you are that she has learned *how* to include specific details so very well. Then, explain that knowing *how* to do something is one part of the job. The next part is learning *why* writers include specific detail and *where* those details matter most. Read the writer's text together, and zero in on one or two places where the details *do* matter most and explain *why*. Now ask the writer to identify another spot where the details matter and have her explain why. When she is able to do that, lead her to identify a spot where she has included details that are not needed. Coach her through a rewrite that will spotlight the significant moments with her details.

Identify Cause

The writer may believe that details are about telling exactly what happened.

Give the Writer Tools to Move Forward

- Ask the writer to talk about what he is writing. Listen for those details missing in print that he layers in during his oral rendition. Take note of how he feels and how he uses his words to signal that. Repeat the language of his oral rendition, and invite him to include it in the text.

- Listen to the writer read her text aloud. Make note of a couple of places where sensory detail would lift the writing. Come back to those places in the text, and ask her to tell you more. Make note as she speaks. Ask questions that will evoke a response requiring sensory details that matter. (For example, don't ask what color the bike was unless it is important for the reader to know. Or, if there was a fire mentioned in the text you might ask her if she smelled smoke or saw flames or smoke.)

Mentor texts:
Bigmama's by Donald Crews
Saving Samantha by Robbyn Smith van Frankenhuyzen
Crow Call by Lois Lowry

Bringing Closure/Endings

9

Most of us have read student writing that runs out of steam, fizzling down to an unsatisfying "The End" or "then I woke up, it was all a dream," or "after that we went home." Finding a way to draw the text to closure that leaves the reader with a sense of ending is a difficult task for inexperienced writers. Perhaps they are setting out on a journey with no destination in mind. It's as if they get sparked by an idea, jump into writing, write until they run out of energy, and then simply stop.

As mentors we guide our writers toward planning for the full journey. We help them consider the ending as they envision the work. This isn't to say they must know the exact language or even precisely how the text will draw to a close, but they need a general notion of where they are going with the writing. So as we confer with writers, let's include a focus on how they imagine drawing the piece to a close. Knowing that will help a writer consider the path as well as the time and energy required to reach the end of this writing journey.

Donald Murray (1990) reminds us that many writers report writing the ending first or beginning with a sense of the ending—they need that destination in mind before they set out on the journey of writing. Some of them actually write the final chapter, the ending scene, or the last lines before writing any other part. Others report that they simply must know how or where the text will end before they can begin. Zinsser (2001) wrote "a good last sentence—or last paragraph—is a joy in itself. It gives the reader a lift, and it lingers when the article is over" (65). Extending that idea, Ralph Fletcher (1993) contends "[t]he ending may be the most important part of a piece of writing. It is the ending, after all, that will resonate in the ear of the reader when the piece of writing has been finished. If the ending fails, the work fails in its entirety" (92).

So, how can we help our less experienced writers move forward? Clark (2011) reminds us that as human beings we know a lot about endings. "Everything that children experience—from travel, to the school year, to stories in books, to movies and television programs, to video games—leaves them with what literary scholar Frank Kermode calls the 'sense of an ending'" (229). So let's tap into that reservoir, and help them recognize the potential of their own experience.

Identify Cause

The writer does not have a clear vision for the text and writes aimlessly without awareness of the need for closure.

Give the Writer Tools to Move Forward

- Ask the writer to tell you a bumper sticker for the draft—that is to state the big idea or message she wants the reader to leave with. Write what she says, read it back to her, and say something like, "So with that idea in mind let's think about your story (essay, report, poem). Where would you end this piece if that is what you want the reader to leave with?"

- Ask the writer to talk with you about the text: "What would you like the reader to remember?" Write down what he tells you. "So let's think together, if you want the reader to remember _____, let's think about how this could end and leave the reader with that idea."

- Ask the writer to think about the text type (all-about, how-to, article, story, memoir) she is writing and her purpose (e.g., to inform, to persuade, to entertain). Write down her responses, and explore with her how texts of that type and with that purpose often end. Scaffold to help her recognize that endings have both a function often tied to the author's purpose and a form often connected to the type of text.

9

Identify Cause

The writer does not have a repertoire of options for ending various types of writing.

Give the Writer Tools to Move Forward

- Ask the writer to think of events or things that end (TV programs, birthday parties, sleepovers, movies, stories, songs, lunch time, recess). Scaffold a conversation that helps him discover his own knowledge of endings. Talk about the routine of lunch, for example. "How do we end lunch every day? If you were writing about how we do lunch each day you would know that is where the piece would end. Knowing that would help you as you start writing. Let's think about your topic. What do you know about how things like that end?"

- Using a set of familiar texts, take at look at the types of endings represented. Together make a list with examples in the writer's notebook. Now, invite the writer to imagine the text she is writing with each of these types of endings. Explore with her how each may look and sound. Leave her with the decision of which would work best for her story.

- Launch a study of endings, and explore the various ways a writer can bring a text to closure.

Identify Cause

The writer lacks or loses focus, leaving the writer unable to find a sense of closure.

Give the Writer Tools to Move Forward

- Ask the writer to return to her original plan and to share with you how she had imagined this text ending. Invite her to read the text aloud to you. As you listen make note of where and how the focus shifts. Ask the writer to tell you what she would like the reader to remember from the text. Show the writer the various "focal points," and ask if one of those will take the reader in the intended direction. This process may require revision to remove extraneous detail that shifted the focus.

- Begin a conversation: "Let's return to your idea for this piece. Before you began the draft, what were your thoughts about how this would go?" Make notes. "So the focus for this piece is _____. Let's read through your draft together. I'll read and pause in a few places. Each time I pause I'd like you to tell me if that bit of the draft is about your focus or not." Bracket the sections that are on target and read those without the distracting bits. Ask her to talk about what would come next and where it should end up.

Identify Cause

The writer's organizing structure doesn't suggest a point of closure.

Give the Writer Tools to Move Forward

- Revisit the writer's plan or vision for the text. Think aloud with her to generate a plot map or outline for the text she is envisioning.

- Ask the writer to name one or two other texts that are like what she has in mind. Examine those texts and make a plot map or outline for each, noting how they are organized. Then, make a plot map or outline for the writer's text using what is written to date. Invite the writer to compare and contrast these maps to spark ideas for finding a way to bring closure.

Opportunities for Study/Mentor Texts: Endings and the Work They Do in the Writing

The opportunity here is to explore endings with attention focused on the *work* the ending is doing in the text. We've listed several for you, hoping that from this list you'll be able to locate a small subset to explore in your classroom. Begin with a few titles, and present them as a read-aloud experience. Share each title two or three times before delving into specific aspects of any book.

As familiarity is gained, lead a discussion about the essence of the book, what it's about, and what they take from it. Return to the closing lines, and note how they bring a sense of closure, saying "good-bye" or "see you again soon" to the reader.

Now invite them to work together with favorite titles they select from independent reading, read-aloud experiences, guided reading, or book clubs. Repeat the process, and note the work being done by the ending in each of those texts. The collective result may be a chart that can serve as a reminder of the work an ending can do when the writer is aware.

9

Endings: *Examples from Professional Writers*			
AUTHOR	TITLE	EXAMPLE FROM TEXT	WHAT IT DOES
Ruby Bridges	*Through My Eyes*	*I know that experience comes to us for a purpose, and if we follow the guidance of the spirit within us, we will probably find that the purpose is a good one.*	The ending is a quote from the author (narrator) that offers a reflection and could be taken as a challenge to the reader.
Marla Frazee	*Roller Coaster*	*Now the ride is over. . . . But at least one of them is planning to ride the roller coaster again . . . right now!*	The ending mirrors the beginning. Opens with tension or anxiety and closes with parallel language and the opposite emotion.

(continues)

Endings: *Examples from Professional Writers (continued)*

AUTHOR	TITLE	EXAMPLE FROM TEXT	WHAT IT DOES
Tony Johnston	*The Harmonica*	*"Play, Jew!" The commandant spat, night after night.* * Night after night I touched the harmonica to my lips. I thought of my father, who had given it to me. Of my mother. . . . I played for them— with all my heart.*	The ending offers a reflection and hope.
Ezra Jack Keats	*Apt. 3*	*Then the dark room filled with wild, happy music. . . . They couldn't wait for tomorrow.*	The ending draws from the cumulative effect of events in the story and shows a change in the characters.
Ezra Jack Keats	*Peter's Chair*	*Peter sat in a grown-up chair. . . ."Daddy," said Peter, "let's paint the little chair pink for Susie . . ."*	The ending reveals a change in thought and action of a character.
Lester L. Laminack	*Saturdays and Teacakes*	*Don't worry, Mammaw. I won't ever forget.*	The ending shows a reflection.
Lester L. Laminack	*Snow Day*	*I CAN'T BE LATE! I'm the teacher!* * Drat! I really needed a snow day.*	The ending contains a surprise that reveals the narrator.
Lester L. Laminack	*The Sunsets of Miss Olivia Wiggins*	*All the while, Miss Olivia Wiggins sat perfectly still, staring at nothing and at everything, all at the same time.*	The ending echoes the language of the opening.

AUTHOR	TITLE	EXAMPLE FROM TEXT	WHAT IT DOES
Helen Lester	*Hurty Feelings*	*As he lumbered away, Rudy called, "Fragility, you're a solid piece of work" . . . stopped short, smiled sweetly, and said, "Why, thank you."*	The ending reveals a change in attitude in the main character.
Helen Lester	*Me First*	*He was just in time to catch the bus. On he scooted—pink, plump, and glad to be last.*	The ending reveals a lesson learned by the character.
Karin Littlewood	*Immi's Gift*	*But this time, something catches his eye, shining in the sand. . . . Then he hangs it around his neck where once he wore a little wooden bird.*	The ending brings the events to a logical but surprising conclusion.
Ella George Lyon	*Come a Tide*	*Now we'll be fine, except in spring . . . hope Grandma won't say, "Children, it'll come a tide."*	The ending closes with a quote from a character and ties back to the opening.
David McPhail	*The Teddy Bear*	*"Thank you," he said to the little boy. "I don't know what I'd do without him."* *"I know what you mean," said the little boy. "I used to have one just like him."* *Then, with his mother and father beside him, he walked back to the corner to wait for the light to change.*	The ending contains a surprise where the character makes an unexpected decision.

(continues)

9

Endings: *Examples from Professional Writers (continued)*

AUTHOR	TITLE	EXAMPLE FROM TEXT	WHAT IT DOES
Derek Munson	*Enemy Pie*	As for Enemy Pie, I still don't know how to make it . . . But I don't know if I'll ever get an answer, because I just lost my best enemy.	The ending reveals a change in thought and action in the character.
Catherine Myler Fruisen	*My Mother's Pearls*	Who do YOU think will wear them next?	The ending poses a question for the reader to ponder.
Pam Munoz Ryan	*When Marian Sang*	Tonight was her debut with the Metropolitan Opera. At long last, she had reached the sun and the moon. The curtains parted . . . and Marian sang.	The ending shows how the character triumphed over a series of obstacles.
Cynthia Rylant	*An Angel for Solomon Singer*	Solomon Singer has found a place he loves and he doesn't feel lonely anymore, and if you are ever near the Westway Café . . . Solomon Singer will smile and make you feel you are home.	The ending offers a solution to the problem presented in the opening.
Cynthia Rylant	*The Old Woman Who Named Things*	From that day on, Lucky lived with the old woman, and he always came when his name was called. . . . And every night Roxanne was sure to make herself plenty wide enough for a shy, brown, lucky dog—and the old woman who named him.	The ending reveals a change in the character.

Endings: *Examples from Professional Writers (continued)*

AUTHOR	TITLE	EXAMPLE FROM TEXT	WHAT IT DOES
Cathryn Sill	*About Insects: A Guide for Children*	*Plate 6* *Insects smell, feel, and sometimes hear through sensory organs called antennae. Antennae are usually located on the front of the head . . .*	The ending contains an afterword that provides more detailed information about each fact presented on the individual spreads. Note: This structure is used in all the books in this series.
Melissa Stewart	*A Place for Bats*	*Sometimes people do things that can harm bats. But there are many ways you can help these special creatures live far into the future.* Note: The book then closes with a list of ways to help, followed by interesting bat facts.	The ending offers a challenge for readers to take action.
Carole Boston Weatherford	*Birmingham, 1963*	Note: The fictional memoir-poem ends with a poetic profile of the four young girls killed in the bombing of the 16th Street Baptist Church. This is followed by an author's note giving the historic facts behind the text.	The ending prompts a moment of reflection and draws attention to the truth of the text.
Tony Wilson	*The Princess and the Packet of Frozen Peas*	*The prince beamed. Pippa beamed back. She had a lovely gap between her two front teeth. "Will you marry me?" . . . "You'll be an UNREAL PRINCESS."*	The ending offers a surprise twist.

Resisting Revision

Many inexperienced writers think of revision as a post-writing inspection. The idea of rewording, reorganizing, deleting extraneous detail, layering in, changing perspectives, trying a different voice or shifting tense, adding dialog, trying a different lead, or tweaking a transition feels like the penalty for not doing it well enough the first time. Perhaps the biggest challenge with revision, then, is to revise our own view of it so we can lead student writers to more positive understandings. Katherine Paterson's perspective is one we find helpful and nonthreatening: "I love revisions. Where else in life can spilled milk be turned into ice cream?" (1995).

If we think of revision as an ongoing process rather than a postwriting inspection, we see it differently. Consider the process of building a home. You begin with some notion of what you hope for. You consult books of home plans, visit homes, and begin to develop your vision for the house you want to build. An architect develops the plan, and a contractor sets the crew to work. You visit the site frequently to monitor the developing home. All through the process you inspect the work and revisit the blueprint. There are times when you see the reality of the developing home and pause. You revisit the plans and alter your original thoughts to create something more pleasing, more useful, or more to your liking. In short, you revise. This process of monitoring as you go is a natural flow in so many areas of our lives. Why then do we teach our student writers to do something other than that?

When we set out to build a house we are purposeful and focused. We have a clear vision of what we expect the outcome to be, yet we remain open to the notion of making changes as we go along. In fact, we expect changes. Anyone who has built a house will tell you there are many changes made throughout the process. Let's think of writing as building a text. We begin with an idea and develop a focus for the project. We proceed with a vision, an intention, a purpose we are working toward. All along the way we pause, inspect, and reflect. We compare what is developing in print with the original vision. From time to time we make decisions to change or fine-tune, to pull back or zoom in. We alter the plan, we adjust, we adapt the vision; we revise. Revision is natural and essential.

Roy Peter Clark (2011) suggests we devote one-third of our writing time and energy to revision. He is not suggesting that it be the last third; instead he recommends that we revise throughout the process. Our experience tells us that revision in many classrooms receives much less than one-third of the time and energy devoted to writing. It is no surprise, then, that student writers are less than enamored with revision because we have not led them to see it as a natural part of the process. However, if we teach our student writers to begin with a plan and to pause throughout the process of developing the text for the purpose of inspection and reflection, we will likely find revision becomes more fluid and productive for them. While we do not believe there is one right way or best way to revise writing, we firmly believe there is one best attitude toward revision and that is to see revision as an opportunity to turn spilled milk into ice cream.

Identify Cause

The writer views revision as a penalty for not having a perfect draft.

Give the Writer Tools to Move Forward

- Show the writer something you have written, and let him see all the revisions you made in the development of the final draft. Explain when and how and why you made each decision. Point out how the final draft was different because of the revisions.

- Invite the writer to recall a time when he was building something with blocks. Ask him to think about changes he made all along the way, figuring out which block would fit next to make what he wanted. Remind him that writing is like building something—along the way you stop to take a look at how it is coming along, and often you make some changes.

Mentor texts:
Hooray for Diffendoofer Day! by Dr. Seuss with Jack Prelutsky and Lane Smith
Arthur Writes a Story by Marc Brown
Author: A True Story by Helen Lester

Identify Cause

The writer is firm in her belief that she has conveyed her intentions and that revision is not needed.

Give the Writer Tools to Move Forward

- Confer with the writer, and ask her to talk about her text: How did you choose this topic? What did you decide to focus on? What would you like your readers to know when they finish? What would you like your readers to feel and think after they have read this? Make notes as she is talking. Now restate her thoughts so you and she have them as a clear guide for rereading her draft. Choose a response to focus on, and reread the draft aloud to her. Pause along the way to consider how the response could guide revision in the text.

Identify Cause

The writer's energy has been expended in the process of producing the draft.

Give the Writer Tools to Move Forward

- Recognize the burst of energy that is expended when a writer gets an idea and sets to work. The rush comes from getting it down on paper and seeing it emerge and take shape. When the writer reaches his stopping point, he may be taxed, physically, emotionally, or both. At this point it may be best to redirect energy to revisit his plan and reread what he has written without pushing for revision unless he initiates it.

- Have a "work in progress" file for each writer. When the writer hits a wall, have him pull a piece from this file to reread, recast, revisit, or revise. The emotional and physical distance from a previously written piece can help to redirect his writing energy until he is ready to refocus on the newly written text.

Identify Cause

The writer has lost enthusiasm for the project.

Give the Writer Tools to Move Forward

- In a conversation with the writer revisit her original interest in the topic. Read through the text with her to determine why she lost enthusiasm for the project. Has she taken on a topic about which she has too little background? Is her focus too broad, leaving her feeling overwhelmed? Is her interest in the topic genuine?

- Revisit the writer's original plan for the text. What had she hoped to create? Did she choose a form not well matched to the topic?

- Consider the questions above. Help her locate resources to broaden her background. Set up an interview with someone who has keen interest and knowledge of her topic.

- Using what you garner from the conversation with the writer, help her find a specific focus for her project.

- Guide her toward a small set of potential mentor texts. Note the form, focus, and structure of these as you help her rekindle her interest and reshape her vision.

Identify Cause

The writer's vocabulary is limited, making word-choice revisions difficult.

Give the Writer Tools to Move Forward

- Help the writer gather a small set of texts related to his topic to build background knowledge. Make note of specific terminology used in these texts. Create a list of words associated with the topic. Create a topic-specific glossary.

- Read aloud to the writer or group, noting the rich language used to convey information, emotions, and perspectives.

- Read the writer's text carefully. Make note of general terms, words that lack specificity (for example, *good*, *nice*, *a lot*, *big*, *heavy*, *fun*). On a clean page in his notebook list these words, leaving a couple of lines between each. Select a small set of mentor texts (picture books, feature articles, poems, letters, essays, blog posts, websites) to read together. Pause to make note of more specific language used in each. At each pause return to the notebook and add synonyms for the words on the list.

Mentor texts:
Farmer Duck by Martin Waddell
Bigmama's by Donald Crews
Bat Loves the Night by Nicola Davies

Identify Cause

The writer thinks of revision as adding detail (needs more techniques for revision).

Give the Writer Tools to Move Forward

- Revisit the options for revision with the writer. Using your own drafts, or the drafts of others, show her examples of rearranging the text, trying a new lead, shifting tense, changing perspective, layering in dialog, removing extraneous information, changing the ending, and replacing general terms with more specific ones.

- Show her texts with a before and after impact. Let her read or listen to an early draft alongside a final draft. Then guide her through noticing the changes. Categorize the changes into different types of revision techniques. Invite her to select a couple to try in her draft.

Identify Cause

The writer does not understand that revision can mean removing details, scenes, or chunks of text to improve clarity.

Give the Writer Tools to Move Forward

- Ask the writer to talk briefly about his topic and the focus he selected for this text. Then ask him to read the text aloud. As he reads, note extraneous details, off-topic segments, or misplaced scenes. As he reaches the end of the text ask if he noticed anything that didn't really fit with the focus he was working toward. Listen to his response, and follow his lead. If he doesn't recognize the extraneous bit, return to one you noted, and explain why it doesn't fit the focus. Then, read the text aloud to him leaving out that bit, and discuss the impact.

- Take a familiar text, and zoom in on a page where the writing is concise and clear. Read that bit aloud with the writer. Then ask the writer to listen as you read and layer in extraneous details. Ask him to talk about the impact of that extra detail. Examine the text together, and talk about the decisions the author may have made to get that crisp, clear text.

Mentor texts:
Crow Call by Lois Lowry
Home Run by Robert Burleigh

Identify Cause

The writer's notion of revision does not include moving segments of text to reorganize or refocus the writing.

Give the Writer Tools to Move Forward

- Some writers need a running start to get themselves focused and on topic. It is not unusual for student writers to meander a bit with front matter that gets them focused. Explain that these lead-up details may actually detract from the focus they intend.

Mentor texts:
Roller Coaster by Marla Frazee
Saturdays and Teacakes by Lester L. Laminack

Identify Cause

The writer has limited understanding of text structures, reducing his options for making revisions that require reorganizing.

Give the Writer Tools to Move Forward

- Before you ask the writer to read her text to you, ask her to restate her topic and focus. Now ask her to place a check mark next to the spot where that focus begins to develop.

Gaining Control Over Conventions

11

Try not to notice that raindrop on the lens of your glasses. Ignore that streak on the windshield where the wiper blade picked up a droplet of oil from the car in front of you. Go ahead, tell yourself you will not look again at the small bit of spinach stuck on the server's tooth when he returns to refill your drink. It's interesting to think about how our concentration is drawn to the "out of place" or the "unexpected" in our everyday lives. It is as if our focus is trained to zoom in on anything that falls outside the norm. So when it comes to reading the work of a developing writer we will naturally zoom in on the wobbly letters, the missing or misplaced punctuation, the unconventional spellings, and the capital letters sprinkled randomly like pepper to spice up a dish.

Noticing the ways a student's writing falls outside the parameters of convention is normal behavior for a teacher. However, our professional judgment is called for in deciding when and how to respond. As hard as it may sound we must make a concerted effort to notice all that is clear and strong and developing in each new text the student writes. Clearly we will notice almost everything that falls outside the parameters of conventions. But we can teach ourselves to keep notes, to reflect on why these errors are happening, and to look past the convention and into the writer's intentions.

Lucy Calkins reminds us to teach the writer, not the writing. We urge you to remember that our focus needs to be on developing the writer, not simply on making any one piece better. So look for patterns of error in the writer's work. Select one or two specifics you believe will move the writer forward. Lead him in small steps toward controlling the conventions of English and slowly build his confidence and competence as a writer. And remember that too much at one time will simply overwhelm a developing writer and most likely cause him to pull back or even shut down.

Move your writers forward; have them write often and much. Give them choice over topic so their writing energies will be fueled by a passion. Having something to say about a topic of great personal importance gives one a reason to write with an audience in mind. Going public, sharing with an audience beyond oneself, calls for clear communication and adherence to the conventions of the culture. In short, function precedes form.

Identify Cause

The writer lacks a general understanding of the purpose of punctuation.

Give the Writer Tools to Move Forward

- Select a text familiar to the writer. Type it in one font and without punctuation. Invite the student to read it aloud. Note whether her voice "adds" punctuation as she reads aloud. Discuss the experience. Next place the original text next to the typed version, and read aloud, noting how punctuation signals the reader and helps to make meaning.

Mentor texts:
Roller Coaster by Marla Frazee
Night in the Country by Cynthia Rylant
I Will Keep You Safe and Sound by Lori Haskins Houran

- Develop a stack of mentor texts, and invite the writer to read with attention to how punctuation is used to help the reader know how the text should sound. Discuss how punctuation helps the text make more sense. Rewrite a favorite part using different punctuation to show how punctuation alters the phrasing, intonation, and meaning.

Identify Cause

The writer's understanding of the uses of the comma is developing or is perhaps tied to his reading behavior as he sees it as a signal to pause when reading.

Give the Writer Tools to Move Forward

- While conferring with the writer focus on one or two ways commas are used to help readers. Turn to a clean page in the writer's notebook, and begin a personal list of how commas help readers make sense. Include the title of one book as an example for each way you list.

Mentor texts:
Zephyr Takes Flight by Steve Light
Ants! Time for Kids
Here Comes Trouble! by Corinne Demas
Brave Squish Rabbit by Katherine Battersby

- Bring a couple of texts (books, articles, essays, etc.) where a comma is used within a compound or complex sentence. Discuss how the punctuation is used to combine shorter, more simple sentences or phrases into one coherent thought.

Mentor text:
Charley's First Night by Amy Hest

- Select three or four texts that allow you to contrast the use of commas to separate a list of items in a series. Explore how each writer may have made that decision by examining the impact it makes upon meaning. A strong, clear example of this contrast can be found in the opening pages of Chapter 3 of *Charlotte's Web* as White describes the smell of a barn by listing all the individual scents connected by "and." A few lines later he uses commas to separate the list of farm implements that can be found in a typical barn.

Mentor texts:
Charlotte's Web by E. B. White (Chapter 3)
Owen by Kevin Henkes (using *and*)
Chitty Chitty Bang Bang by Ian Fleming (very long list using *and*, p. 1)
Ants! Time for Kids (items in a series)

Identify Cause

The writer understands quotation marks through a reader's lens. She knows these marks signal that someone is talking. However, control over when to include them in her writing is still developing.

Give the Writer Tools to Move Forward

- Select three to five texts including picture books, articles, essays, poems, etc., where the writer has made use of dialogue. Study how each of the authors uses quotation marks to reveal when a character is speaking or when someone is being quoted. Give the students time to study the punctuation use and draw attention to how other punctuation is used in conjunction with quotation marks.

Mentor texts:
Owen by Kevin Henkes
Small Bunny's Blue Blanket by Tatyana Feeney
Splat Says Thank You! by Rob Scotton
Charley's First Night by Amy Hest
Frog and Toad by Arnold Lobel
The Book of "Unnecessary" Quotation Marks: A Celebration of Creative Punctuation by Bethany Keeley
If You Were Quotation Marks by Molly Blaisdell

11

Identify Cause

The writer has been taught that an exclamation mark is used to show excitement or shouting and overgeneralizes the appropriate use of this punctuation mark.

Give the Writer Tools to Move Forward

- Select an entry from your notebook and show the writer something you are excited about. On a sheet of draft paper, write a paragraph based on your notebook entry. As you write, sprinkle in exclamation marks liberally. Now ask the writer to read your draft with the energy called for by the exclamation marks. Read the draft aloud to her, and discuss what sounds odd and why. Together work back through the draft, sentence by sentence. Remove and replace all but one of the exclamation marks. Discuss how you decide where the exclamation mark works best.

Mentor texts:
Exclamation Mark by Amy Krouse Rosenthal and Tom Lichtenheld
Oh, What a Christmas! by Michael Garland
Splat Says Thank You! by Rob Scotton
Yo! Yes? by Chris Raschka
If You Were an Exclamation Point by Shelly Lyons

- Gather three to five books from the classroom library, and invite the writer to read each and place a sticky note on any page where the author used an exclamation mark. Return to the set, and revisit each usage of the exclamation mark. Read the segment aloud together, and invite the writer to make a theory about why the author made the decision to include the mark. Work together to generate a statement that will help guide the writer in a more controlled and appropriate use of the exclamation mark in his writing.

Identify Cause

The writer recognizes the difference in the formation of a comma, a semicolon, and a colon but doesn't understand the difference in the functions.

Give the Writer Tools to Move Forward

- Show the writer how to combine two independent clauses from her text using a semicolon. It may also help to revisit the function of the comma.

- Gather a stack of mentor texts (information, fiction, poetry, picture books, articles, or essays), and invite the writer to work with a partner or small group to search for several examples of the use of commas and semicolons. Use two different colored sticky notes to flag the examples. Working as a team, generate a theory to explain how a writer decides whether to use the comma or the semicolon.

- Consider pulling a stack of mentor texts and having writers explore the use of the colon to see if they can deduct the how and why of the punctuation.

Mentor texts:
Eats, Shoots & Leaves by Lynne Truss
Ants! Time for Kids

Identify Cause

The writer has seen the dash used in many texts but has no parameters for its use.

 ## Give the Writer Tools to Move Forward

- Authors use the dash often and for various reasons. Return to the stack of mentor texts, and invite the writer to explore the different ways authors have used the dash. Suggest that he share his findings with the group.

Mentor text:
Zephyr Takes Flight by Steve Light

Identify Cause

The writer has had repeated exposure to the ellipsis (dot, dot, dot) in the reading workshop but understands very little about how to use it in writing.

Give the Writer Tools to Move Forward

- Pull several mentor texts that show the use of the ellipsis, and point out that the ellipsis has only three dots unless it is at the end of the sentence where a period makes it looks like you've used four. Read selected segments of these texts showing the use of the ellipsis, and invite the writer to deduct the function it serves. Test his theory with additional segments. Then work together to generate a statement guiding the use of the ellipsis in his writing.

Mentor texts:
Splat Says Thank You! by Rob Scotton
Roller Coaster by Marla Frazee
Exclamation Mark by Amy Krouse Rosenthal and Tom Lichtenheld
Zephyr Takes Flight by Steve Light
Lucky Ducklings by Eva Moore
I Will Keep You Safe and Sound by Lori Haskins Houran
Owen by Kevin Henkes
Brave Squish Rabbit by Katherine Battersby
Small Bunny's Blue Blanket by Tatyana Feeney

Additional Mentor Texts to Consider

Punctuation:

The Punctuation Station by Brian P. Cleary

Punctuation Takes a Vacation by Robin Pulver

Punctuation Celebration by Elsa Knight Bruno

Twenty-Odd Ducks: Why, Every Punctuation Mark Counts! by Lynne Truss

Commas:

Eats, Shoots & Leaves: Why, Commas Really Do Make a Difference! by Lynne Truss

If You Were a Comma by Molly Blaisdell

Question Marks:

If You Were a Question Mark by Shelly Lyons

Periods:

If You Were a Period by Nicholas M. Healy

Apostrophes:

The Girl's Like Spaghetti: Why, You Can't Manage without Apostrophes! by Lynne Truss

Greedy Apostrophe: A Cautionary Tale by Jan Carr

If You Were an Apostrophe by Shelly Lyons

Glossary

Mentor/Mentor Text: The words *mentor text* are batted around in the world of writing instruction more than a shuttlecock in a badminton tournament. So let's be clear about what we mean when we say *mentor text* in *The Writing Teacher's Troubleshooting Guide*. We see a mentor as a guide, a coach, a tutor who has vested interest in the student's well-being. A mentor would not take control but rather would guide you in selecting a path, lead you in analyzing your options, and help you learn to recognize patterns in your behavior that are pulling you away from your goal. A mentor would coach you in trying out options as you discover your way. A mentor would broaden your horizons and offer new options you could not have considered with only your limited view.

Consider the coach of a sports team sharing video clips of another team. Together the coach and the players view and analyze the plays of the other team. Together they explore the other team's moves and ponder the decisions behind those moves as they look for insight as to how to improve. Together they make a plan to try out something new, to see how it feels and how it works. In that scenario the coach is using the video clip as a mentor text. The coach selected that particular clip specifically because it demonstrates options he believes will broaden his players' strategies and build their skills. The coach intentionally gathered his team and had them examine and think through selected moves of another team.

Likewise, a writing teacher is a trusted counselor, guide, coach, and tutor for her writers. Like the coach of a sports team, a writing teacher keenly observes her writers and notes where each is reaching a plateau in development. A writing teacher often gathers the work of other writers who have accomplished what her students are on the cusp of understanding. Like the coach showing his players the moves of another team, the writing teacher uses the texts of another writer to highlight selected writing moves she believes will open new options for her students.

Together with her students a writing teacher examines the text, notices what the writer has done, and ponders the decisions about why and how the writer accomplished each move. All this is done in an effort to broaden students' repertoire of strategies and deepen their understanding of how writers work. All this is done to make students better writers.

Mentor texts, then, are books, articles, essays, websites, and more that are carefully selected because they hold the potential to expand a writer's repertoire of strategies. Therefore, writing teachers must have a collection of texts they know well enough to pull pertinent examples from as the need arises. The mentor text has potential that will be untapped without that insight.

Revise/Revision: To look again; to look over again in order to improve; to study again; to make a new, amended, improved, or up-to-date version of . . .

Revision in *The Writing Teacher's Troubleshooting Guide* means that writers return to their plan and revisit their intentions to be clear about what they hoped to convey before, during, and after beginning a draft or rewrite. That original intention or vision is held in mind as writers read and reread what they have written. This rereading may result in changing the text or may result in modifying the vision. Either is acceptable. The point is to sharpen the focus, tighten the writing, remove the extraneous, layer in elaboration or explanation as needed, and create the text that best matches the writers' intention.

So during revision a writer may choose to:

- Reread to make sure it sounds right, looks right, and makes sense
- Reread for focus on one topic
- Reread to be sure the end connects to the topic
- Reread and picture the text like a movie to check whether anything is missing
- Check each scene, and decide whether the illustration supports or extends the text
- Add words or language ("fancy" words, more specific words, feelings, emotions, description, images, thoughts, dialog)
- Reorganize the text, checking for logical sequence or progression from beginning to end
- Read aloud to someone else, and ask him or her to tell what makes sense or doesn't. Ask what he or she notices. Ask him or her to summarize the text with a bumper sticker.
- Add a scene to elaborate, extend, or reveal a character
- Rechunk segments to bring logic to the organization of the text

- Delete a scene to bring logic to the flow of the text
- Replace narration with dialog to reveal what the characters are thinking and feeling

Setting: Location, weather, emotional tone, situational context, frame of reference . . .

Setting is an essential aspect of writing that provides the narrator, the characters, and the events with a context, a framework within which to exist. Setting can tell us where we are and how it feels to be there, what the weather is like, and whether we should be fearful or cautious or run headlong into what lies ahead. Setting helps us understand tone and mood. It helps us know the character or the situation. Setting helps establish the atmosphere for emotions and feelings to rise. At times the setting is merely a required backdrop against which the action or events are played out—a stage, if you will. Yet, other times the setting is an essential part of the story itself. Some contend that setting can almost be a character. If, for example, your writer is working on a story about playing catch with a friend, it *could* happen almost anywhere there is ample space (park, school playground, ball field, vacant lot, backyard). However, if an essential part of the story is a broken window on the neighbor's front porch, her reaction to that broken window, and

the narrator's feelings of guilt and attempts for redemption, the setting, then, becomes an important part of the text itself. Less experienced writers may get caught up in the action and focus their writing energy on capturing sequential events or facts with no awareness of how setting influences those details. That broken window, for example, may take on more significance on a clear, cold winter afternoon than a mild spring morning. Likewise, being lost in the desert for forty-five days with no food or water has a different feel than being lost in your best friend's house for twenty minutes. Setting is so much more than where it happens.

Transition: passage from one scene, setting, event, conversation, subject, or place to another . . .

Transitions are not easy. The absence of a transition in writing leaves the reader with a jolt like driving along a smooth ribbon of pavement and hitting a stretch of gravel road at seventy miles per hour. Writing teachers often lament the absence of transitions in their students' writing, so let's be clear what we mean by the term.

In *The Writing Teacher's Troubleshooting Guide* we use the word *transition* to mean the intentional use of language to bring closure to one segment, scene, or event and connect it to or lead into the next. Think of it as the threshold between rooms as you move through a house or as the couplings that link train cars together.

Voice: It seems that many of us have a notion that voice is a complex and elusive quality in writing. Donald Murray (2013) reminds us that as children we learn how to shift and select voice to match situations. We don't have one all-occasion voice; rather we select and adjust our voice as the situation or audience shifts.

Voice, then, is that quality of writing that enables a writer to bring personality to the surface for the reader. A writer doesn't write with only one voice; rather he adjusts voice to match the character or situation. An impetuous, impulsive, hyper character would have a different sound from a thoughtful, careful, reflective character. A somber situation such as a funeral would call for a different voice than a festive event such as a parade or a New Year's Eve countdown. The voice of an essay on global warming would be different from the voice of a narrator leading you through a kid's birthday party. The point to remember is that a single writer may produce any of these voices to match the demands of the task.

Ruth Culham says that voice is the "tone and tenor of the piece—the personal stamp of the writer . . . the force behind the words that proves a real person is speaking and cares about what is being said . . . the heart and soul of writing" (2010, 142).

Ralph Fletcher says, "When I talk about voice, I mean written words that carry with them the sense that someone has actually written them. Not a committee, not a computer: a single human being. Writing with voice has the same quirky cadence that makes human speech so impossible to resist listening to" (1993, 68).

From our perspective in *The Writing Teacher's Troubleshooting Guide*, voice is that quality that helps to establish the tone and bring the reader into the situation through the words we choose, the sentences we make from those words, and how we arrange those sentences into paragraphs as we tell story, build an argument, slant an essay, or unfold a poem.

Recommended Professional Resources

Chapter 1: Nothing to Write About

Bender, J. 2007. *The Resourceful Writing Teacher.* Portsmouth, NH: Heinemann, Chapter 9.

Calkins, L. 1994. *The Art of Teaching Writing.* Portsmouth, NH, Heinemann.

Culham, R. 2005. *6 + 1 Traits of Writing.* New York: Scholastic, Chapter 3.

Fletcher, R. 1993. *What a Writer Needs.* Portsmouth, NH: Heinemann.

Fletcher, R. 2012. *Mentor Author, Mentor Texts.* Portsmouth, NH: Heinemann, 31–32.

Glover, M. 2009. *Engaging Young Writers.* Portsmouth, NH: Heinemann.

Graves, D. H. 1994. *A Fresh Look at Writing.* Portsmouth, NH: Heinemann, Chapter 3.

Davis, J., and S. Hill. *The No-Nonsense Guide to Teaching Writing.* Portsmouth, NH: Heinemann, 84–85.

Olness, R. 2005. *Using Literature to Enhance Writing Instruction.* Urbana, IL: International Reading Association, Chapter 4.

Ray, K. 2010. *In Pictures and In Words.* Portsmouth, NH: Heinemann.

Routman, R. 2005. *Writing Essentials.* Portsmouth, NH: Heinemann, Chapter 2.

Spandel, V. 2012. *Creating Young Writers.* Boston: Pearson, Chapter 3.

Chapter 2: Exploring a Topic

Bender, J. 2007. *The Resourceful Writing Teacher.* Portsmouth, NH: Heinemann. Chapter 2.

Fletcher, R. 1993. *What a Writer Needs.* Portsmouth, NH: Heinemann, Chapter 13.

Routman, R. 2005. *Writing Essentials.* Portsmouth, NH: Heinemann.

Chapter 3: Finding a Vision

Bomer, K. 2010. *Hidden Gems.* Portsmouth, NH: Heinemann.

Calkins, L. 1994. *The Art of Teaching Writing.* Portsmouth, NH: Heinemann, Chapter 15.

Chapter 4: Finding a Focus

Anderson, C. 2005. *Assessing Writers.* Portsmouth, NH: Heinemann.

Bender, J. 2007. *The Resourceful Writing Teacher.* Portsmouth, NH: Heinemann, Chapter 3.

Lane, B. 1999. *Reviser's Toolbox.* Shoreham, VT: Discover Writing, Chapter 2.

Chapter 5: Developing a Lead

Bender, J. 2007. *The Resourceful Writing Teacher.* Portsmouth, NH: Heinemann, Chapter 7.

Fletcher, R. 1993. *What a Writer Needs.* Portsmouth, NH: Heinemann, Chapter 7.

Lane, B. 1999. *Reviser's Toolbox.* Shoreham, VT: Discover Writing, Chapter 1.

Routman, R. 2005. *Writing Essentials.* Portsmouth, NH: Heinemann, 13, 17, 19, 148, 228, 309.

Chapter 6: Establishing a Context or Setting

Bender, J. 2007. *The Resourceful Writing Teacher.* Portsmouth, NH: Heinemann, Chapter 5.

Fletcher, R. 1993. *What a Writer Needs.* Portsmouth, NH: Heinemann, Chapter 10.

Laminack, L. 2007. *Cracking Open the Author's Craft.* New York: Scholastic.

Chapter 7: Wandering Off on a Tangent

Fletcher, R. 1993. *What a Writer Needs.* Portsmouth, NH: Heinemann, Chapter 4.

Chapter 8: Controlling Details

Laminack, L. 2007. *Cracking Open the Author's Craft.* New York: Scholastic.

Olness, R. 2005. *Using Literature to Enhance Writing Instruction.* Urbana, IL: International Reading Association, Chapter 4.

Chapter 9: Bringing Closure/Endings

Bender, J. 2007. *The Resourceful Writing Teacher.* Portsmouth, NH: Heinemann, Chapter 8.

Fletcher, R. 1993. *What a Writer Needs.* Portsmouth, NH: Heinemann, Chapter 8.

Laminack, L. 2007. *Cracking Open the Author's Craft.* New York: Scholastic.

Lane, B. 1999. *Reviser's Toolbox.* Shoreham, VT: Discover Writing, 35, 39.

Chapter 10: Resisting Revision

Bender, J. 2007. *The Resourceful Writing Teacher.* Heinemann: Portsmouth, NH: Heinemann, Chapters 15–18.

Calkins, L. 1994. *The Art of Teaching Writing.* Portsmouth, NH: Heinemann, Chapter 4.

Calkins, L. 1991. *Living Between the Lines.* Portsmouth, NH: Heinemann, Chapter 7.

Davis, J., and S. Hill. *The No-Nonsense Guide to Teaching Writing.* Portsmouth, NH: Heinemann, Chapter 9.

Graves, D. 1994. *A Fresh Look at Writing.* Portsmouth, NH: Heinemann, Chapter 3.

Hale, E. 2008. *Crafting Writers, K–6.* Portland, ME: Stenhouse, Chapter 5.

Heard, G. 2002. *The Revision Toolbox.* Portsmouth, NH: Heinemann.

Heard, G. 1995.*Writing Toward Home.* Portsmouth, NH: Heinemann, 121.

Lane, B. 1999. *Reviser's Toolbox.* Shoreham, VT: Discover Writing, Chapter 9.

Routman, R. 2005. *Writing Essentials.* Portsmouth, NH: Heinemann, 156–60, 318–19, 321–22, 335.

Spandel, V. 2012. *Creating Young Writers.* Boston: Pearson, Chapters 11–13.

Chapter 11: Gaining Control over Conventions, Editing

Anderson, J. 2005. *Mechanically Inclined.* Portland, ME: Stenhouse, Grades 6–12.

Bender, J. 2007. *The Resourceful Writing Teacher.* Portsmouth, NH: Heinemann, Chapter 19.

Calkins, L. 1994. *The Art of Teaching Writing.* Portsmouth, NH: Heinemann, Chapter 18.

Hale, E. 2008. *Crafting Writers, K–6,* Portland, ME: Stenhouse, Chapter 5.

Davis, J., and S. Hill. *The No-Nonsense Guide to Teaching Writing.* Portsmouth, NH: Heinemann, 89.

Olness, R. 2005. *Using Literature to Enhance Writing Instruction.* Newark, DE: International Reading Association.

Routman, R. 2005. *Writing Essentials.* Portsmouth, NH: Heinemann, 230–35 and Chapter 10.

Sloan, M. 2009. *Into Writing.* Portsmouth, NH: Heinemann, Chapter 8.

Spandel, V. 2012. *Creating Young Writers.* Boston: Pearson, Chapters 13–14.

Wilde, S. 2012. *Funner Grammar.* Portsmouth, NH: Heinemann, Grades 3–8.

Chapter 11: Gaining Control over Conventions, Punctuation

Anderson, J. 2005. *Mechanically Inclined.* Portland, ME: Stenhouse.

Bender. J. 2007. *The Resourceful Writing Teacher.* Portsmouth, NH: Heinemann, 18–21, 24–27, 76–78, 81–82, 194–97, 200, 214–23, 218.

Culham, R. 2005. *6 + 1 Traits of Writing.* New York: Scholastic, Chapter 8.

Dorn, L., and C. Soffos. 2001. *Scaffolding Young Writers*. Portland, ME: Stenhouse, 13, 14, 21, 51.

Dudley-Marling, C., P. Paugh. 2009. *Struggling Writers*. Portsmouth, NH: Heinemann, 31–32, 44–45, 113, 130–32.

Graves. D. 1994. *A Fresh Look at Writing*. Portsmouth, NH: Heinemann, Chapter 3.

Graves, D., and P. Kittle. 2005. *Inside Writing: How to Teach the Details of Craft*. Portsmouth, NH: Heinemann, 84.

Hale, E. 2008. *Crafting Writers, K–6*. Portland, ME: Stenhouse, 2, 19, 50, 63–67, 68, 70–78, 79–80, 153, 178, 181.

Heard, G. 1995. *Writing Toward Home*. Portsmouth, NH: Heinemann, 125.

Routman, R. 2005. *Writing Essentials*. Portsmouth, NH: Heinemann, 13, 66, 69–70.

Wilde, S. 2012. *Funner Grammar*. Portsmouth, NH: Heinemann, Chapter 2.

Additional Professional Resources:

Using the Writer's Notebook

Calkins, L. 1991. *Living Between the Lines*. Portsmouth, NH: Heinemann, Chapter 4.

Davis, J., and S. Hill. *The No-Nonsense Guide to Teaching Writing*. Portsmouth, NH: Heinemann, 84, Chapter 5.

Dudley-Marling, C., and P. Paugh. 2009. *Struggling Writers*. Portsmouth, NH: Heinemann, 38, 82, 83.

Fletcher, R. 1996. *Breathing In, Breathing Out*. Portsmouth, NH: Heinemann.

Harwayne, S. 2001. *Writing Through Childhood*. Portsmouth, NH: Heinemann, 43–46, 50, 58–61, 78, 116, 122–23, 305–306.

Using Mentor Texts

Calkins, L. 1994. *The Art of Teaching Writing*. Portsmouth, NH: Heinemann, Chapter 3, Section 15.

Davis, J., and S. Hill. *The No-Nonsense Guide to Teaching Writing*. Portsmouth, NH: Heinemann, 108–18, Chapters 2 and 12.

Fletcher, R. 2013. *What a Writer Needs*. Portsmouth, NH: Heinemann.

Laminack, L. 2007. *Cracking Open the Author's Craft*. New York: Scholastic.

Laminack, L., and R. Wadsworth. 2005. *Learning Under the Influence of Language and Literature*. Portsmouth, NH: Heinemann, Chapter 5.

Olness, R. 2005. *Using Literature to Enhance Writing Instruction*. Urbana, IL: International Reading Association.

Parsons, S. 2005. *First Grade Writers*. Portsmouth, NH: Heinemann.

Ray, K. 1999. *Wondrous Words*. Urbana, IL: International Reading Association.

Ray, K. 2010. *In Pictures and In Words*. Portsmouth, NH: Heinemann.

Writing Process

Dorn, L., and C. Soffos. 2001. *Scaffolding Young Writers*. Portland, ME: Stenhouse, 2–7, 11, 37–47, 78.

Dudley-Marling, C., and P. Paugh. 2009. *Struggling Writers*. Portsmouth, NH: Heinemann, 4–5, 34–37, 43.

Hindley, J. 1996. *In the Company of Children*. Portland, ME: Stenhouse, 45–56, 66–69, 76–78.

Routman, R. 2005. *Writing Essentials*. Portsmouth, NH: Heinemann, 8, 14, 15, 35–40, 124, 178.

Sloan, M. 2009. *Into Writing*. Portsmouth, NH: Heinemann, 177–82.

Structure and Organization

Corgill, A. 2008. *Of Primary Importance*. Portland, ME: Stenhouse.

Culham, R. 2005. *6 + 1 Traits of Writing*. New York: Scholastic, Chapter 4.

Fletcher, R. 1993. *What a Writer Needs*. Portsmouth, NH: Heinemann, Chapter 11.

Heard, G. 2002. *The Revision Toolbox*. Portsmouth, NH: Heinemann, Chapter 4.

Olness, R. 2005. *Using Literature to Enhance Writing Instruction*. Urbana, IL: International Reading Association, Chapter 5.

Routman, R. 2005. *Writing Essentials*. Portsmouth, NH: Heinemann, 13, 23, 173, 190–92, 228–29.

Developing Voice

Culham, R. 2005. *6 + 1 Traits of Writing*. New York: Scholastic, Chapter 5.

Fletcher, R. 1993. *What a Writer Needs*. Portsmouth, NH: Heinemann, Chapter 6.

Heard, G. 2002. *The Revision Toolbox*. Portsmouth, NH: Heinemann, Chapter 5.

Olness, R. 2005. *Using Literature to Enhance Writing Instruction*. Urbana, IL: International Reading Association, Chapter 6.

Routman, R. 2005. *Writing Essentials*. Portsmouth, NH: Heinemann, 13, 29, 147, 223.

References

Allison, Dorothy. 2009. "Place." *The Writer's Notebook: Craft Essays from Tin House*. Portland, OR: Tin House Books.

Clark, Roy Peter. 2011. *Help! For Writers*. New York: Little Brown and Company.

Culham, Ruth. 2010. *Traits of Writing: The Complete Guide for Middle School*. New York: Scholastic.

Dillard, Annie. 1989. *The Writing Life*. New York: HarperCollins.

Fletcher, Ralph. 1993. *What a Writer Needs*. Portsmouth, NH: Heinemann.

Gotham Writers Workshop. 2003. *Writing Fiction*. New York: Bloomsbury.

Lamott, Anne. 1994. *Bird by Bird*. New York: Anchor Books [Doubleday].

Murray, Donald M. 1989. *Expecting the Unexpected*. Portsmouth, NH: Heinemann.

———. 1990. *Shoptalk: Learning to Write with Writers*. Portsmouth, NH: Heinemann.

———. 2013. *The Craft of Revision*, 5th Edition. Boston: Wadsworth Cengage Learning.

Paterson, Katherine. 1995. *A Sense of Wonder: On Reading and Writing Books for Children*. New York: Penguin.

Welty, Eudora. 1984. *One Writer's Beginnings*. Cambridge, MA: Harvard University Press.

Zinsser, William. 2001. *On Writing Well*, 25th Anniversary Edition. New York: Quill (HarperCollins).